THE A-Z OF THE
SEWING MACHINE

THE A-Z OF THE SEWING MACHINE

Maxine Henry

B.T. Batsford Ltd, London

First published 1994

© Maxine Henry 1994
All line artwork © Deborah Matthews

Typeset by Servis Filmsetting Ltd, Manchester
and printed in Great Britain
by The Bath Press, Bath

Published by
B.T. Batsford Ltd
4 Fitzhardinge Street
London W1H 0AH

A catalogue record for this book is available from the British Library

ISBN 0 7134 7324 X

CONTENTS

ACKNOWLEDGEMENTS 6

INTRODUCTION 7

APPLIQUÉ 8

BINDING 11

BRAIDS AND CORD 14

BUTTONS 18

BUTTONHOLES 19

CHOOSING A MACHINE 21

CUTWORK 24

DARNING 27

DIFFICULT FABRICS 28

DO'S AND DON'TS 30

ELASTIC 32

EMBROIDERY (FREE) 35

EMBROIDERY (PRE-SET) 41

FAULTS 43

FEET 46

GATHERING 48

HEMS 51

HOOPS 56

LACE 58

MAINTENANCE 61

NEEDLES 63

OVERLOCKERS 66

PATCHWORK 68

PIPING 72

PRESSURE CONTROL 75

QUILTING 76

ROULEAU 80

SEAMS 82

SMOCKING 85

STITCHES 91

STRETCH FABRIC SEWING 94

TENSION 96

THREADS 98

TIPS 99

TOP STITCHING 102

TUCKS 103

TWIN NEEDLES 107

ZIPS 109

NOTES 112

ACKNOWLEDGEMENTS

I would like to de...dicate this book to my husband, Stuart, who for
most of our married life, has had to put up with lost buttons and
hanging-down hems. I love challenging sewing, but hate mending!
I would also like to thank him for his tolerance, when so often
sewing has taken precedence over meals and housework.

I am also indebted to the New Home (Janome) Sewing Machine
Company for their help. They loaned me a Memory Craft 8000
sewing machine. I enjoyed using it so much that I could not bear to
part with it!

All line drawings are by Deborah Matthews and Maxine Henry.

INTRODUCTION

While some people cannot resist opening the fridge for a quick nibble as they pass, I cannot resist trying out a new technique on my sewing machine (especially if I am just about to vacuum, iron or dust!!). Try leaving your machine set up for a couple of weeks and set aside half an hour a day to systematically try out all its different attachments and stitches. You will quickly become familiar with various feet and stitches and subsequently, when you need to use them for garments or projects, you will obtain better results.

Once you have built up a rapport with your sewing machine, using it will become an addiction. There were times when I felt sorry for colleagues who went home from work only to watch television, when I was rushing home to get started on a new project on my sewing machine.

I have tried to make this book simple to use by giving step-by-step instructions with numerous settings and diagrams. The contents are arranged in alphabetical order for ease of reference.

I hope that by reading and working through this book you gain confidence and pleasure from using your machine.

The sewing machine Before reading this book familiarize yourself with the basic parts and functions on your sewing machine

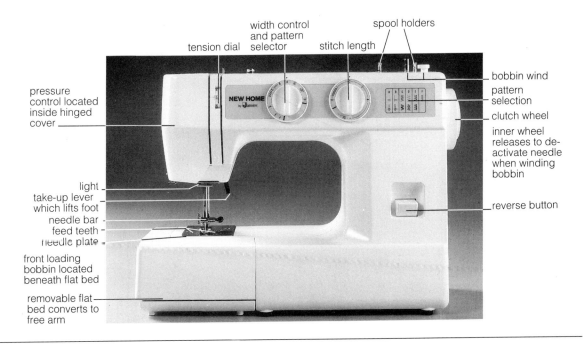

- tension dial
- width control and pattern selector
- stitch length
- spool holders
- pressure control located inside hinged cover
- bobbin wind
- pattern selection
- clutch wheel
- inner wheel releases to de-activate needle when winding bobbin
- light
- take-up lever which lifts foot
- needle bar
- feed teeth
- needle plate
- reverse button
- front loading bobbin located beneath flat bed
- removable flat bed converts to free arm

NEW HOME

APPLIQUÉ

Appliqué is the technique of cutting out fabric shapes and sewing them down onto a background fabric to form a design. Highly decorative, it is one of the most versatile crafts and you can sew it onto all fabrics including knitwear and leather. Plain items can be decorated and personalized, it can look distinctive on fashion garments and can be used with stunning effects on soft furnishings. Beads, fabric paint and embroidery are also often used in conjunction with appliqué.

Appliqué is normally sewn using an embroidery hoop – do not be put off by this. Using the hoop actually makes sewing easier and the background fabric remains flat. The only exceptions are when wadding is used beneath the background fabric (the motifs are applied and quilted in one operation), or when sewing appliqué on stretch fabric or knitwear. In this case the knitted fabric is stabilized on the back with stitch-and-tear Vilene before sewing commences. In general the colour of the sewing thread used matches the cut-out shape not the background fabric. When working an intricate design in appliqué it may be necessary to pin your shapes in place, but be careful where you position the pins: if the design is cut from satin etc. the pin marks will show. I use pins because I find tacking threads get caught under the foot of the machine. Bondaweb can be used to hold the fabric shapes in place before stitching, but it gives a 'flat' appearance to the work, and if you are not very careful small shapes are apt to move whilst they are being pressed in place. This can be fatal if it is an eye or a nose!

The design can be cut from cotton, polycotton, satin, taffeta, silk etc. – all good fabrics to use, but avoid loosely woven or knitted fabrics. If any of the fabrics you are using are likely to shrink, wash them first. When making a large item, e.g. a quilt, it is easier to work in small sections and sew them together later. If you have not sewn appliqué before, frame up a spare piece of fabric and have a test run. If you have problems seeing the outline of your design because the foot is in the way, see Tips No. 10, p. 100.

METHOD 1 – SIMPLE APPLIQUÉ
(Appliqué Perse)

In this method whole motifs are cut from pre-printed fabric, e.g. flowers or birds. You should stabilize the fabric *before* cutting by ironing fusible interfacing (iron-on Vilene) onto the back of the

printed fabric. After cutting the shapes, lay them onto a background fabric, and when you are satisfied with your design, put the background fabric in a hoop and sew down the motifs using satin stitch.

1 Set the machine as shown above.

2 Press iron-on Vilene onto the back of the pre-printed fabric. Always iron the Vilene onto the fabric before cutting out the shapes. This ensures a good seal on the cut edge.

3 Arrange the motifs onto the background fabric and pin in place.

4 Frame up the fabric (see under Hoops, p. 56).

5 Satin stitch the motifs in place (for satin stitch see under Stitches, p. 91). The motifs will look more lifelike if they are not just stitched around the edge. If, for example, you are stitching a flower (fig. 1), outline each petal separately. If the back petals are sewn first, the stitching round the top petals will cover where the back stitches start and stop.

If small spaces are formed between the motifs these can be cut away to form cutwork with appliqué (see under Cutwork, p. 24).

METHOD 2 – REVERSE APPLIQUÉ (Découpé)

It is possible to work reverse appliqué using two to seven different layers of coloured fabric. (The more fabrics used the more difficult the appliqué is to handle). Three layers would be a good choice for a beginner. Suitable designs can be created by folding and cutting shapes out of paper. You will find this method of appliqué particularly suitable for intricate designs which have lots of small areas.

1 Set the machine as shown in Method 1.

2 Choose between two to seven different coloured fabrics and place them one on top of the other. The top layer has the design drawn on the right side (use dressmakers' carbon paper to transfer the design to the fabric).

3 Frame up the fabrics or hold in place with pins.

4 Outline the design with satin stitch (see under Stitches, p. 91), sewing through all layers (fig. 2).

5 Then cut away the layers exposing the different colours (figs. 3-4).

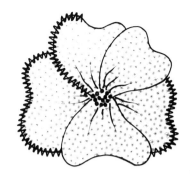

Fig. 1 *The back petals are shown first*

Fig. 2 *Outline the design with satin stitch, sewing through all layers of fabric*

Fig. 3 *Carefully cut away the top fabric to reveal the second layer of fabric*

Fig. 4 *Cut away the two top layers to reveal the third layer of fabric*

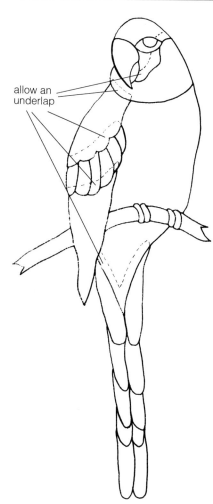

allow an
underlap

Fig. 5 *Mark the underlap allowance on your tracing. Transfer the dotted lines onto your fabrics using dress makers' carbon paper. Then cut out the shapes*

NOTE:

On larger designs it may be necessary to move the hoop several times.

Appliqué will be more thoroughly dealt with in a subsequent book on Appliqué and Thread Painting.

METHOD 3 – APPLIQUÉ, CREATING AND WORKING YOUR OWN DESIGN

Draw the design on tracing paper even if you are drawing free hand. This enables you to turn the drawing over if you need a mirror image. Also it is easier to use up small scraps of fabric. You can see through the paper to line them up.

1 Set the machine as shown in Method 1.

2 Choose the fabrics to be used and press iron-on Vilene onto the back of all the fabrics.

3 Transfer the part of the design which is relevant to each piece of fabric using dressmakers' carbon paper (instructions for use under Cutwork, Method for Working Cutwork, p. 25).

4 Cut out the shapes. If you are cutting a motif out of several different coloured fabrics an underlap must be allowed. Raw edges must not just butt up to each other – one must underlap the other (*fig. 5*). This can be marked on the tracing paper to make cutting out easier.

5 When all the pieces of the design have been cut out, frame the background fabric ready for sewing (see under Hoops, p. 56).

6 Arrange the part of the design to be sewn, in the hoop. Build up all layers before stitching commences.

7 Apply the shapes to the background fabric using satin stitch. Smooth the shapes flat with your left hand as you sew.

BINDINGS

Bindings are used to neaten raw edges, and are most successful if they are made from the true bias of the fabric (cut diagonally across the grain line), as they lay flatter and stretch around curves. Ready-made bias binding in cotton, satin and patterned fabrics can be purchased, but often to obtain just the right colour we need to make our own.

TO CUT AND MAKE BIAS BINDING

Method

1 Mark a square on your fabric with the straight of grain laying across the top and down the side.

2 Fold the two opposite corners A and B together making a diagonal fold across the square (*fig. 6*). Then press the fold.

3 Open out the fabric and cut narrow bias strips parallel with the crease (*fig. 7*).

4 Join the ends of the strips together making crosswise seams to form a long length of binding (*fig. 8*).

5 Press the seams open. Then press the side edges of the binding inwards towards the wrong side (*fig. 9*).

The bias binding is now ready to attach to a raw edge. An accessory can be bought from haberdashery shops which simplifies turning in and pressing the edges of the bias strips. A special foot may also be used to attach the bias binding (*fig. 10*). It folds the binding and attaches both edges enclosing a raw edge, one on top and one below, simultaneously. This foot gives a very neat finish.

Fig. 10 *Bias binding foot*

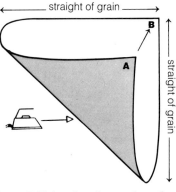

Fig. 6 *Fold A to B and press along the diagonal fold*

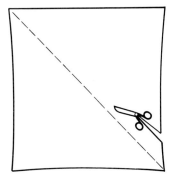

Fig. 7 *Cut narrow strips of fabric parallel with the crease*

Fig. 8 *Join the strips together making crosswise seams*

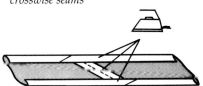

Fig. 9 *Press seam and edges to the wrong side to form the binding*

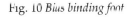

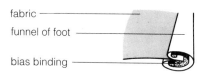

fabric
funnel of foot
bias binding

Fig. 11 *This shows the fabric and binding inserted into the funnel of the foot*

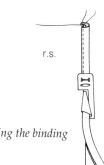

r.s.

Fig. 12 *Attaching the binding*

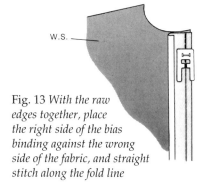

w.s.

Fig. 13 *With the raw edges together, place the right side of the bias binding against the wrong side of the fabric, and straight stitch along the fold line*

Fig. 14 *Fold the binding enclosing the raw edges and stitch in place on the right side*

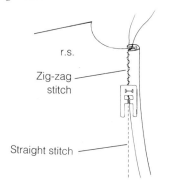

r.s.

Zig-zag stitch

Straight stitch

ATTACHING BIAS BINDING

Method 1 – Using a binding foot (fig. 10)

1 Set the machine as shown.

2 The binding is fed down the funnel of the foot with the fold on the right hand side (*fig. 11*).

3 The raw edge of the fabric is fed flat into the groove in the left hand side of the funnel.

4 The binding may be attached with either straight stitch (*fig. 12*) or a narrow zig-zag stitch.

Method 2 – Using a general purpose foot to stitch both edges of the binding

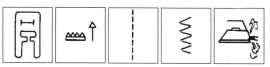

1 Set the machine as shown.

2 Place the two raw edges together with the right side of the bias binding against the wrong side of the fabric. Straight stitch down the fold line (*fig. 13*).

3 Press the binding towards the seam.

4 Fold the binding over the seam to the right side of the fabric.

5 Stitch the binding in place from the right side using a very narrow zig-zag stitch (*fig. 14*). (The binding will just cover the line of straight stitching).

Method 3 – Using a general purpose foot to stitch one edge, hand stitching the other

1 Set the machine as shown.

2 Place the two raw edges together with the right side of the bias binding against the right side of the fabric.

3 Seam together, using a straight stitch, along the fold line of the bias binding (*fig. 15*).

4 Press the binding towards the seam.

5 Fold the binding over the raw edges to the wrong side of the fabric; and catch down, by hand, just covering the row of straight stitching (*fig. 16*).

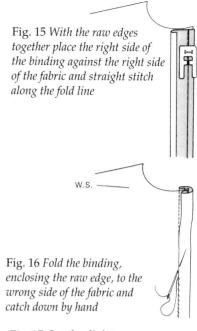

Fig. 15 *With the raw edges together place the right side of the binding against the right side of the fabric and straight stitch along the fold line*

CONTINUOUS LAP BINDING

This is used to bind a slit, e.g. binding a front neck opening prior to sewing on a collar, or binding the opening at the bottom of a sleeve before the cuff is sewn in place.

Method

1 Set the machine as shown.

2 Cut the binding on the bias (see Bias Binding, p. 11) Twice the length of the slit is needed.

Fig. 16 *Fold the binding, enclosing the raw edge, to the wrong side of the fabric and catch down by hand*

Fig. 17 *Cut the slit between the stay stitching.*

3 Mark the slit and stay-stitch round the mark before it is cut, tapering the stitching towards the bottom of the mark.

4 Cut the slit and open outwards to lay flat (*fig. 17*).

5 With right sides together pin the binding along the slit edge and stitch in place (*fig. 18*).

6 Press the binding towards the seam.

7 Fold the binding over the raw edges. Turn under a narrow hem and hand stitch in place on the back of the fabric.

8 Press, then lap the binding over at the bottom of the opening and stitch in place.

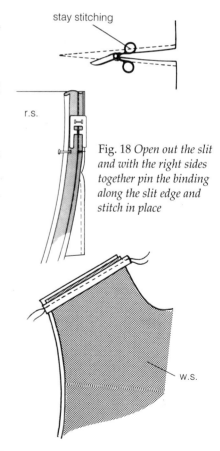

Fig. 18 *Open out the slit and with the right sides together pin the binding along the slit edge and stitch in place*

FLAT BINDINGS

Flat seam binding, tape or ribbon can also be used as a binding. It is cut or woven with the edges parallel to the grain line. It can be used to bind an edge which has been cut exactly on the straight of the grain line or to stabilize an edge. For example, you can sometimes sew it along a shoulder seam, when using a stretch fabric, to prevent the seam from stretching (*fig. 19*).

Fig. 19 *Stitch flat binding in place across a shoulder seam, on a stretch fabric, to prevent the seam from stretching*

BRAIDS AND CORDS

A variety of braids can be made using the sewing machine. If you need a braid to match a garment or soft furnishings it is often easier, and less time consuming, to make one. In most cases you go to the shops with high hopes when trying to match a particular colour, but often come home tired and disillusioned.

A SEWN CORD BRAID

Method

In order to sew this braid you will need a braiding foot. Again these vary with make. They may look like either of the following:

Fig. 20 *A seven-cord braiding foot*

Fig. 21 *A three-cord braiding foot*

• Up to seven cords can be threaded down through the holes in this foot (*fig. 20*). The short cut ends of cord lay under the back of the foot and the long lengths lay in front of the foot.

• Up to three cords can be sewn down using this foot (*fig. 21*). The cords are threaded through the three small tunnels and the short ends lay beneath the back of the foot. (This foot can also be used to advantage when sewing down shirring elastic).

A variety of cords can be used, e.g. crochet cotton, metallic thread, silky viscose cord, wool or thin ribbon. This type of braid looks particularly effective when sewn down the fronts of an edge-to-edge jacket or waistcoat, (especially if some of the colours in the jacket/waistcoat are used for the cords). It can also be used on jacket cuffs, round the edge of pocket flaps, for outlining a sailor type collar or defining a border on a cushion or bedspread. It looks particularly smart as an edging for lampshades.

Three-step zig-zag is an ideal stitch to use to sew the braid down, but some embroidery stitches also make interesting braid. You will need to experiment with the stitches which are available on your particular machine.

Making the braid

1 Set the machine as shown.

2 Set the width of stitch to cover the number of cords used. When using three-step zig-zag the stitch length will be set on about one third of the maximum length, e.g. if your stitch length goes from 0–6 set it on 2.

3 Mark the fabric where the braid is to be stitched. (The braid is made and stitched in place in one operation).

4 Thread the selected cords into the foot (a combination of different cords and colours can be used in a braid).

5 Position the fabric under the foot, laying the cords along the fabric in front of the foot, and stitch in place (*fig. 22*).

It is possible to sew round curves with the braid, but not small tight curves.

RUCHED RIBBON BRAID

Method

This is a very decorative method of ruching (gathering ribbon). The widest ribbon which can be used is dependent on the maximum sideways swing of your machine e.g. if your needle will sew a three-step zig-zag measuring almost 1 cm across you can use up to 1 cm wide ribbon. The ruched braid, because it is made from ribbon, tends to look luxurious and rather feminine. It has many applications – here are a few suggestions:

• As a decorative edge to a bedroom lampshade.

• Sewn round a cushion it makes a pleasant change from piping.

• It can be sewn to outline shapes, e.g. diamonds, on a quilt.

• It can be sewn along seam lines.

• It looks very decorative if sewn on wedding or evening dresses, either as shoulder straps or edging a neckline or frill.

• It can be sewn on christening gowns or round the inside of a christening bonnet.

• It can be sewn into whirls to make decorative rosettes.

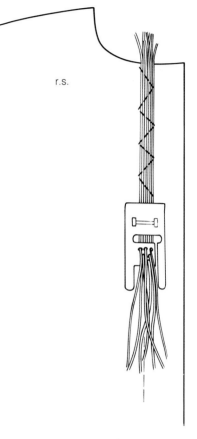

r.s.

Fig. 22 *The cords are stitched in place on the right side of the fabric*

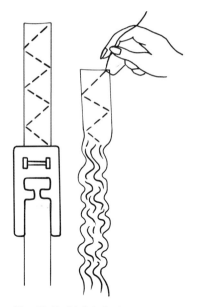

Fig. 23 (Left) *Stitch along length of ribbon using three-step zig-zag stitch*

Fig. 24 (Right) *Pull up the bobbin thread to produce small curves along the edges of the ribbon*

Ruching the ribbon

1 Set the machine as shown.

2 Make a small test sample setting the stitch width just slightly narrower than the ribbon, and the stitch length to the shortest stitch which will enable you to pull up the ribbon into gathers. The amount of ribbon used is two and a half times the required finished length.

3 With a matching thread stitch the entire length of ribbon needed (*fig. 23*).

4 Pull the bobbin thread, ruching up the ribbon (*fig. 24*). Small curves will appear along each edge of the ribbon.

5 The braid can then be applied. I like to sew it down by hand stitching along the centre of the ruched braid.

RUSSIA BRAID

Russia braid is a versatile narrow silky braid which is cheap to buy and comes in a variety of colours. It has a groove in the centre of two cords, and is attached using a straight stitch, the needle following this central groove. The narrow cords on either side of the Russia braid can be unravelled and pulled to make the braid bend (*fig. 25*). It can be used to make a dramatic design if black braid is sewn down flat forming a pattern, perhaps on the yoke, cuffs or front of a jacket or dress (*figs. 26-27*).

This type of braid is also ideal to use as stems for flowers in appliqué or embroidery, but most of all it makes an easy narrow piping for dressmaking (see under Piping, p. 73).

You may be able to buy a special foot or guide for your machine

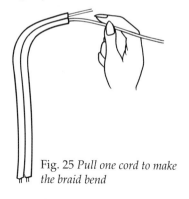

Fig. 25 *Pull one cord to make the braid bend*

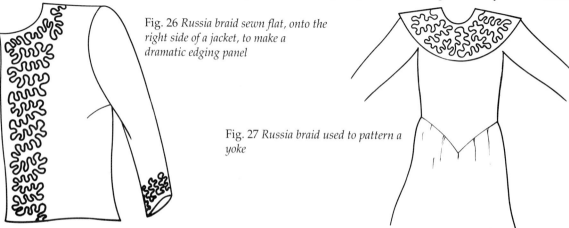

Fig. 26 *Russia braid sewn flat, onto the right side of a jacket, to make a dramatic edging panel*

Fig. 27 *Russia braid used to pattern a yoke*

which makes sewing a cord on easier. The cord is automatically lined up with the needle. On some makes this will also accommodate a narrow braid (*fig. 28a*) .

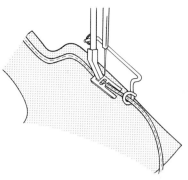

Fig. 28a *A cording attachment is used to guide a narrow cord or braid*

RICK-RACK BRAID

This wavey-edged braid tends to cheapen a garment when sewn down flat but it can look totally different if it is used to pipe a seam or edge the back of a hem (see under Piping and Hems, p. 74).

CORDS

You can sew round cords directly in place. Thick cords should be sewn along one side only, using a zig-zag stitch which just catches the side of the cord (*fig. 28b*). You may need to experiment with different feet and the pressure control will need reducing where applicable (see under Pressure Control p. 75).

Fig. 28b *To attach a thick cord sew a small zig-zag stitch along one side of the cord*

Narrow cords are sewn down, again using the zig-zag stitch. This time sew the stitch right across the cord, feeding it through a cording foot or guide. This automatically guides the cord down the centre of the foot making it possible to machine freely – when you turn on the fabric the cord will follow (*fig.29*). You could, for example, easily write your name or sew quite complicated corded patterns.

For Rouleau, see under Rouleau, p. 80, and for Wrapped Cords see under Free Emboidery, p. 37.

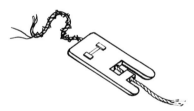

Fig. 29 *Sewing fine cord using a cording foot and zig-zag stitch*

BUTTONS

SEWING BUTTONS ON USING THE MACHINE

Many people do not like sewing buttons on by machine, but I find it is a very neat method of attaching them, especially if you are making a blouse and will need to sew on as many as ten buttons.

Machines will sew on buttons with either two or four holes but it is easier and quicker to choose buttons which have just the two holes in them. Most machines have a special foot for holding the button in place – consult your machine manual.

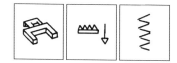

1 Set the machine as shown.

2 Having marked the position of the buttons place the first button on the fabric under the foot of the machine. Lower the foot carefully to hold the button in place.

3 Manually turn the balance wheel downwards and towards you to check that the needle is entering the holes in the button cleanly. Test each side. Adjust the zig-zag stitch if necessary.

4 Sew about ten stitches or so. Some machines have a finishing off facility where the needle sews up and down in the same hole several times to fasten off.

5 If your button has four holes in it repeat the process with the other two holes.

6 If you require a slight shank to your button lay a pin on top of the button between the holes and sew over the pin (*fig. 30*). Remove the pin when stitching is complete.

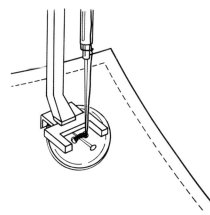

Fig. 30 *Sewing on a button using a pin for the shank*

Once you know the zig-zag width setting to use you will find very little variation in distance between the holes in large or small buttons.

Buttonholes

Different machines have different methods of making buttonholes so it is hard to generalize. I have explained some of the more common methods below.

MANUAL BUTTONHOLES

These tend to occur on older swing needle machines. With this type of buttonhole the fabric needs to be turned after one side of the buttonhole has been stitched.

AUTOMATIC BUTTONHOLES

There are various types:

- Four-step buttonholes

With a four-step buttonhole each phase is activated separately and is normally stitched as follows:
1 left side
2 bar tack
3 right side
4 second bar tack

- Two-step buttonholes

In this case the buttonhole is stitched as follows:
1 sews one side and one bar tack
2 sews the other side and bar tack

- One-step buttonholes

The most up-to-date and often more expensive machines sew this kind of buttonhole. The complete buttonhole is sewn in one operation and in most cases the size of the buttonhole is dictated by the size of the button you place in the buttonhole foot.

When sewing an automatic buttonhole where the machine is sewing one side of the buttonhole forwards and the other side of the buttonhole backwards, the density of the stitches vary from side to side. When you know your machine well, you can compensate for this by adjusting the stitch length for one side of the buttonhole to even it up.

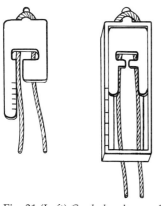

Fig. 31 (Left) *Cord placed around the hook on a buttonhole foot, ready to sew a corded buttonhole*

Fig. 32 (Right) *Cord in place ready for sewing a corded buttonhole using a buttonhole shoe*

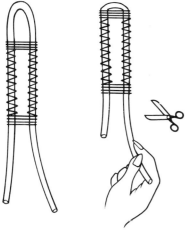

Fig. 33 (Left) *A corded buttonhole showing the cord loop*

Fig. 34 (Right) *The cord is pulled to fit the buttonhole and the surplus cord is cut off close to the bar tack*

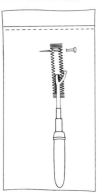

CORDED BUTTONHOLES

On some machines the buttonhole foot has a hook on the back of the foot and grooves on the underside of the foot (*fig. 31*). On others the hook is on the buttonhole shoe (*fig. 32*).

To make a corded buttonhole, place a length of thin cord under the foot, around the hook and back under the foot again. Sew the buttonhole in the usual manner, but do not hold the cord whilst sewing (fig. 33). Remove the fabric from the machine and pull the two ends of the cord to eliminate the loop formed (fig. 34). (This loop will reinforce the buttonhole so have it at the end which gets the most wear).

A corded buttonhole is used on thicker fabrics. It is bolder and gives a more tailored look to the garment. It can be used on suits and coats, etc.

If a very thin cord is used corded buttonholes can be sewn on stretch fabrics. It helps to prevent the buttonhole from stretching. For Rouleau button loops see under Rouleau (p. 80).

TIPS FOR PRODUCING A GOOD BUTTONHOLE

- Always use your buttonhole foot.

- Always make a test buttonhole on a double thickness piece of the fabric being used.

- Always start with the bottom buttonhole on a garment.

- Always cut the buttonhole *after* stitching.

- On some thick or loosely woven fabrics it may be necessary to stitch round the buttonhole twice.

- If you are not sure whether to make horizontal or vertical buttonholes it is probably safer to make horizontal ones.

- Vertical buttonholes are normally only used on loose fitting garments, because they tend to come undone if there is any strain on them.

- A buttonhole generally looks neater if an interfacing has been used between the two layers of fabric.

- When cutting the buttonhole place a pin across the far end of the buttonhole and slit open with a stitch unpick (*fig. 35*). This way the pin prevents you overcutting and slicing through the bar tack!.

Fig. 35 *Place a pin across the far end of the buttonhole to prevent cutting through the bar tack!*

CHOOSING A SEWING MACHINE

A sewing machine is a very personal piece of equipment, so when choosing a new machine, spend time looking at the various makes, talk to friends to see how they rate their machines and, most important of all, try the machines out in the shops before you buy. Do not worry about looking foolish if the machines at first seem rather complicated. It is far better to make a mistake at the shop, in front of someone you do not know, than it is to make a rushed decision by buying the wrong machine and discover your mistake later at home, when it is too late to do anything about it.

Remember to take samples of the types of fabric which you usually sew on. The fabrics used in the shops will be easily handled fabrics, which give the stitches a neat appearance. All machines will cope well with these. All machines will not cope well with lycra, for example, and you may be buying your machine to sew lycra skating costumes, or you may be wanting to sew loose covers, so take along some stiff, thicker fabrics and see how the various machines cope. Any shop with a helpful attitude will help you choose a machine suited to your needs and will probably help with any queries in the future. If the shop is unhelpful do not buy from them, they are probably only after your money, and once the sale is made will not provide any aftersales service.

It is not necessary to choose the most expensive machine, but in most cases, I would avoid the cheapest, most basic machines. A middle-of-the-range machine is fine. When choosing bear in mind that machines manufactured in Europe will cost far more than comparable machines manufactured in the Far East. A machine which can cope with most types of sewing should include the following stitches: straight stitch, zig-zag, blind hem, stretch straight stitch, stretch zig-zag, scallop, three-step zig-zag, automatic buttonhole, and possibly stretch overlock and double overlock if you are going to be using a lot of stretch fabrics.

Fig. 36 *A smooth outline is achieved using a versatile width control*

The machine should have a width control which is versatile and can be set anywhere on its range. This enables you to taper the width of stitch gradually, e.g. when tapering satin stitch a smooth outline will be achieved.

If the machine has perhaps only four pre-set widths, it will be limiting when tapering a satin stitch – the outline will be stepped.

Fig. 37 *A width control which only has a few limited preset widths will produce a 'stepped' outline*

The machine should be a free-arm machine. (This means fabrics can pass completely round the sewing bed of the machine). It should convert to a fairly large flat bed, as a small flat bed will not support a hoop. I would require the machine to stitch well without a foot on and with the feed teeth dropped. Ask for this to be demonstrated. Also ask to see the machine sew over a very thick seam, and look for missed stitches or the machine grinding to a halt before the seam!

Only choose a machine with embroidery stitches if you are prepared to pay more for it. If funds are limited it is better to go for a machine with fewer stitches, one which has a good quality straight stitch and zig-zag. After all, they are the stitches you are likely to use ninety nine percent of the time!

I have seen cheap machines which look impressive, sewing up to 100 embroidery stitches, but they had a very irregular straight stitch. Having said that, if you like embroidery, some of the new computerized machines have wonderful satin stitch embroidery facilities, with large multi-coloured designs. These intricate designs can be up to 12.5 cm in size, and as many as five colours can be used in any one design. They make the small outline patterns which we are used to pale into insignificance!

Once you have decided on a machine, ask if a basic range of accessories is kept in stock. Also ask how long the model you are interested in has been on the market – a new model may be coming out shortly. In which case, you would expect the one you are interested in to be reduced, or you may prefer to wait for the new more up-to-date machine. Be cheeky, and ask if the one you are interested in is to be reduced in the next sale!! It can be very annoying to find after paying full price that, a few weeks later it has been reduced.

If you are not interested in having a demonstration or aftersales service and know exactly which machine you wish to buy (maybe a friend has one which you have used and liked), you can quite often buy a machine mail order. Usually the prices are considerably lower but you do not get the service you will get from a reputable shop.

It can sometimes be confusing when you hear terms such as electronic foot control or computerized machine. Below I have tried to provide a simple explanation of some of the more common terms.

A basic zig-zag (or swing needle) machine

This just means that in addition to the machine needle sewing straight stitch forwards and backwards, it also sews from side to side creating a zig-zag stitch. These machines place greater emphasis on manual operation and you have more knobs to adjust to change the stitches. This is usually the cheapest end of the market, but never the less good results are often obtained with this type of machine.

An automatic machine

An automatic machine will have the facility to sew more complicated stitches with fewer adjustments, e.g. a stitch which requires the machine to go forwards and backwards, and from side to side – once selected – will be sewn automatically.

Electronic foot control

This just means that the machine is capable of sewing slowly without losing needle penetration. This type of machine is especially good for sewing thick fabrics.

An electronic machine

We are now in the 'world of the microchip', and some machines contain tiny computers: the stitch is often chosen by the touch of a button, penetration of the needle is good, and the foot control is sensitive. The stitch selection is much greater, sometimes including letters and numbers. Some machines have the facility to link different stitches or patterns together. The stitches are all fully automatic, but you have the option to change their size. Electronic machines are easy to operate and cope well with a large variety of fabrics, and they are usually in the middle price bracket.

Computerized machines

These are the Rolls-Royces of the sewing machine world, and if you are lucky enough to own one I hope you enjoy it, and use it often.

It is difficult to be brief when extolling their many virtues – they are so varied and they do so much, but here goes: these machines have an abundance of practical and decorative stitches displayed, which can be sewn at the touch of a button or pad. They have a memory, patterns can be linked together, or a name programmed. These can be sewn and if necessary they can be re-called, on some models, days later! The machine often indicates which foot to use, some will even flash a message on a small screen if you have made an error, e.g. if you have not put the take-up lever down! Some have the facility for elongating designs or mirror imaging them. Needle penetration is good and speed very controllable – sewing one stitch if necessary. Some will sew on their own, you program in the design, set the machine going, and it will sew the design by itself and stop when the design is completed. It even stops if the thread breaks! Though these machines may look complicated, they are often simple to use with good results almost guaranteed. They are, however, the most expensive of the machines.

CUTWORK

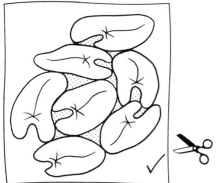

In machine cutwork, gaps formed by the design are cut away. The gaps are created by intertwined shapes outlined with satin stitch. The background fabric between the shapes is cut away *after* stitching has been completed. The design is stitched using a hoop. It is very important not to cut away any of the gaps until all the stitching has been worked. Do not choose a design which has large gaps or one which only creates very narrow bands of fabric between the gaps.

Fig. 38 is an example of a good design.

Fig. 39 is an example of a poor design which creates large areas to be cut away divided by narrow bands of fabric, these will eventually pull away.

It is possible to combine cutwork with appliqué. The fabric shapes are first cut out and then arranged on the main fabric forming small gaps between them. The shapes are then applied to the backing fabric using satin stitch and the gaps formed are cut away. When working appliqué, always wash the fabrics first or use the same type of fabric for the background fabric and for the cut out shapes. This eliminates shrinkage.

Fig. 38 A good design: the areas to be cut away are small and are joined by wide bands of fabric

Fig. 39 A poor design: the areas to be cut away are large and they are only separated by narrow bands of fabric

Method for working machine cutwork

Draw your design onto tracing paper. It is a good idea to cut the tracing paper to the size and shape of the area you wish to fill, e.g. the size needed for the corner of a table cloth or a triangular infill in the front of a blouse. If you which to make a cutwork collar use the pattern pieces as a guide for the shape. Once you have the shape it is easier to draw a balanced design to fill it. The design is transferred onto the right side of the fabric using dressmakers' carbon paper, (sometimes called tracing paper). Office carbon paper can be used but dressmakers' carbon paper comes in assorted colours including white which shows up well on dark fabrics. Remember if you are making a small item in cutwork, e.g. a collar or a table centre-piece, to allow enough fabric to go into a hoop. The excess fabric can be cut off when stitching has been completed. If the area of cutwork to be sewn is large, the hoop may have to be moved several times.

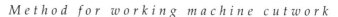

TRANSFERRING THE DESIGN

1 Transfer the design (*fig. 40*) by laying the fabric right side uppermost on a hard surface. Lay the carbon paper, coloured side down, on top of the fabric. Lay the tracing paper on top of the carbon paper. With a very hard pencil outline the design. You will need to press hard, and I find an empty ballpoint pen marks well. The design should now appear on the fabric.

Fig. 40 The collar shape and design are transferred onto the fabric using dressmakers' carbon paper

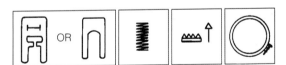

2 Set the machine as shown.

3 Set the stitch width to about halfway and the stitch length to just above 0. (The sideways sewn stitches should lay almost touching each other to form a smooth solid line of satin stitch). Do not be tempted to push the fabric through the machine to speed things up. Satin stitch moves through very slowly.

4 Frame up the fabric. (For further instructions see under Hoops, p. 56). Place the larger ring on the table. Lay the fabric over the ring, right side up with the design central. Push the smaller ring inside the large ring. Pull the outside fabric until the fabric in the hoop is taut. Tighten up the screw.

5 Satin stitch round the drawn shapes (*fig. 41*). Machine embroidery thread gives a smooth shiny appearance to the sewing.

Fig. 41 The fabric is framed in the hoop and the design is outlined using satin stitch

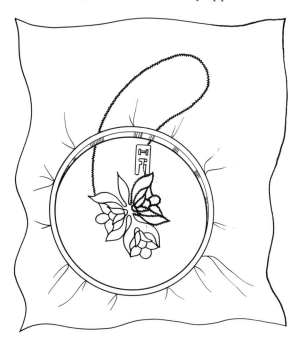

Fig. 42 Only when you have completed all the stitching should you carefully cut away the shaded areas

6 When you have finished sewing remove the work from the hoop and cut away the gaps using small sharp scissors with curved blades. You may find it helpful to mark the areas to be cut away with a water soluble pen (*fig. 42*). (I've known students to be overkeen and cut away the wrong area!).

Cutwork may be worked on a variety of fabrics, but loosely woven and stretch fabrics are unsuitable. Very fine fabrics need to be sewn with very thin embroidery thread or silk. Suitable fabrics are: cotton, polycotton, linen, cotton twill, silk, satin, taffetta and calico.

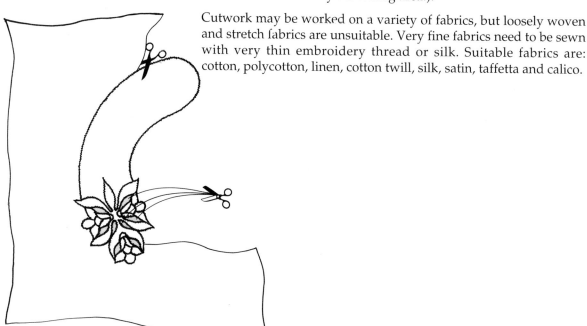

DARNING

Mending is almost a thing of the past as everything seems to be disposable today, but times change so I have included a small section on darning.

Method 1 – To mend a cut or tear

Assuming that the surrounding fabric is not worn or damaged:

1 Set the machine as shown.

2 Iron a patch of iron-on Vilene under the tear making the torn edges meet.

3 Set the stitch width on the widest setting and the stitch length between 0-1.

4 Working from the right side, centre the torn edges under the foot, and sew together. This stitch makes a strong neat join.

Method 2 – To darn a worn area

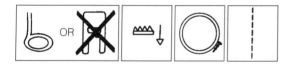

1 Set the machine as shown.

2 You may find darning easier if you frame the area to be stitched (see under Hoops, p. 56).

3 Lower the take-up lever.

4 Turn the balance wheel anticlockwise whilst holding the top thread, to bring the bobbin thread through the surface of the fabric.

5 Hold the edge of the hoop. Sew whilst moving the hoop backwards and forwards. Moving the hoop quickly will produce long stitches, slowly will produce short stitches.

6 Work over the fabric until all worn areas have been darned.

NOTE:

If the area to be darned is very worn you will need to back it with a reinforcing fabric (either a lining fabric, or a small piece of the same fabric). You can hold it in place with Bond-a-Web.

NOTE:

Some machines do not need a darning foot. Work the darning as for Free Embroidery, p. 35.

DIFFICULT FABRICS

Fig. 43 *A straight stitch foot with central hole*

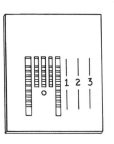

Fig. 44 *A straight stitch needle plate*

TO SEW VERY FINE FABRICS

When sewing straight stitch on very fine fabrics the fabric is apt to be taken down through the needle plate, thus jamming the machine. It often helps to change to a straight stitch foot (*fig. 43*) and straight stitch needle plate (*fig. 44*).

Both of these have a small circular hole in them rather than a wide oval aperture. You may also need to increase the pressure by turning to a higher number on the pressure control. Also use a short stitch length, as a stitch which is too long will cause the fabric to pucker. Do not forget to use a fine needle, and always sew on a double thickness of fabric when testing the stitch.

If you have changed to a straight stitch foot and needle plate it is advisable to change back as soon as your stitching is completed. Never put the machine away with them on, as you may forget and turn to zig-zag. The needle will break and the needle plate will be scored.

When neatening a raw edge on a fine fabric use three step zig-zag stitch to prevent the edge from curling up and forming a ridge. If the fabric is very fine a French seam may be more appropriate (see under Seams, p. 82).

TO SEW SLIPPERY FABRICS

You can sew on slippery fabrics more easily by using a roller or walking foot. These are also useful for sewing two different fabrics together, e.g. velvet and satin, as the feet help to feed the fabrics evenly through the machine (i.e. at the same rate). Some machines also have stick-on teflon feet which are stuck on the bottom of the foot. These teflon stickers help to grip slippery fabrics, and are also useful for sewing plastic coated fabrics and imitation leathers.

TO SEW LEATHER

Leather can sometimes 'stick' to the needle plate. To help it through the machine lay a strip of Stitch-and-Tear Vilene under the leather, and it may also be necessary to place another strip on the top of the leather to lay directly under the foot. The leather then passes freely through the machine and the Vilene tears away after stitching. Remember to use a leather needle and to lengthen the stitch.

TO SEW STRETCH FABRICS

Always loosen off the pressure control (turn to a lower number) when sewing stretch fabrics. This will eliminate the fabric being stretched as it passes under the foot which can cause 'wavy' seams. Take care not to pull or push the fabric through the machine. Use a synthetic thread and a ball point needle, and always sew with a stretch stitch. If your machine does not have stretch stitches, use a very narrow zig-zag stitch instead of a straight stitch for the seams. This will give the seams some elasticity. Some modern stretch fabrics are especially difficult to sew, mainly the silky ones: the needle tends to bounce off the fabric. Try adjusting the tension and experiment with different types and thicknesses of thread until you achieve a satisfactory seam. A new needle or a perfect stitch needle will often help. If your machine is the type which allows for several needle positions move your needle nearer to the edge of the foot. Note that this is only applicable when sewing straight stretch stitch.

TO SEW VELCRO

Even though Velcro is not exactly a fabric it can be difficult to sew. The soft side is sewn as normal, but the side with the stiff hooks is a little more difficult. Try sewing it on with a zig-zag stitch, just catching the edge of the Velcro. It is often easier to sew if the pressure is reduced (see under Pressure Control, p. 75). If you are fastening an overlap with Velcro always stitch the soft piece of Velcro to the back of the overlap, and the stiff piece to the front of the underlap. The stitching on the back of the soft piece always looks neater.

DO'S AND DON'TS

The ideal arrangement is to have a sewing area where your machine can stay set up – you will use it more frequently and become much more confident with it. Before starting to sew, here are some useful do's and don'ts:

DO'S

- Do make sure you are perfectly comfortable and that you are sitting at the right height for the work table.

- Do have plenty of space around the left hand side of your machine.

- Do have a good light and not sit where you cast a shadow over your work.

- Do be positive, and assume that any projects tackled will be easily mastered.

- Do turn the balance wheel downwards and towards you if your machine sounds laboured as you start to sew – it will lengthen the life of the motor.

- Do clean, oil (where applicable) and do general maintenance on your machine regularly. Always turn off the motor first.

- Do relax – enjoy your sewing. It can be fun!

- Do open your bobbin area and operate the balance wheel manually so you can see how the needle thread and the bobbin thread react with each other. This will help you to understand the working of your machine.

- Do take your machine manual to bed with you – it makes fascinating bedtime reading!

- Do use the correct foot for the job, it will take less time and give a neater finish.

- Do remember practice makes perfect!

- Do leave a scrap of fabric under the foot when the machine is not in use, and leave the foot down.

DON'TS

- Don't rush and take short cuts – they always end up taking more time!

- Don't rest your foot on the foot pedal when you are not actually sewing – it will heat up and you will damage your machine.

- Don't switch your machine on and off at the socket. Always use the switch on the machine.

- Don't pull or push your fabric through the machine. Always let it feed through at its own pace. If it does not feed through freely the pressure may need adjusting or the machine may need a service.

- Don't leave your accessory box where the family can use it – small screwdrivers are apt to disappear!

- Don't be tempted to buy a remnant just because it is cheap, and make sure you really like the fabric not the price – it may end up in a cupboard for years!

- Don't use a pin magnet near an electronic or computerized machine.

- Don't forget to change your needle to suit the fabric being sewn, or after every two garments.

ELASTIC

ATTACHING FLAT ELASTIC

Method 1

You can attach narrow flat elastic by sewing it directly onto the fabric (no casing is necessary). This method is not suitable for elastic which is much wider than the sideways swing of the needle.

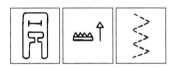

1 Set the machine as shown – (you may need to reduce the pressure).

2 Cut the elastic to the required length allowing for the seam.

3 Position the elastic onto the wrong side of the fabric and pin one end onto the seamline. Pin the other end onto the opposite seamline. (If you are attaching a long length of elastic it will be necessary to pin at intervals between. An easy way to do this is to divide your fabric into four and mark, then divide your elastic into four and mark. Match the marks and pin together).

4 Stitching needs care: hold both ends of the elastic so that it stretches across the width of the fabric (*fig. 45*). (Again if you are sewing a long length of elastic just stretch the elastic between the start and the first pin, then between the first and second pin and so on). Whilst stretching the elastic, stitch in place. Take care not to pull the fabric through the machine, and let it feed at its own pace. Stitch to the end of the elastic.

This method ensures that the fullness of the fabric is evenly distributed, and it is less bulky than using a casing (*fig. 46*). To attach a flat wide elastic using this method follow the same instructions but use a straight stitch. Sew several parallel rows along the elastic depending on its width (*fig. 47*). When you are attaching elastic in the round, e.g. around a waistband, use the free arm on your machine.

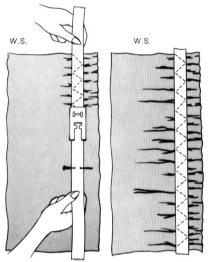

Fig. 45 (Left) *Stretch the elastic to fit the fabric and stitch with care*

Fig. 46 (Right) *When using this method the fullness of the fabric is evenly distributed*

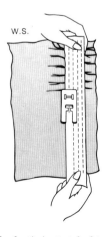

Fig. 47 *The wide elastic is stretched to fit the fabric and straight stitched*

Method 2 – Inserting narrow flat elastic by making a casing

This method is not suitable for elastic which is wider than standard width bias binding.

1 Set the machine as shown.

2 Make a casing on the line where the elastic is needed by sewing standard width bias binding or tape, flat to the wrong side of the fabric.

3 Cut the elastic to the length required allowing for the seam.

4 Using a bodkin or small safety pin thread the elastic through the casing. It is a good idea to pin the end of the elastic to the casing when you start to thread (*fig. 48*) as it sometimes disappears into the casing! If you are crossing seams make sure your seams are pressed very flat first, as this makes threading past them easier.

5 When the elastic is inserted sew the ends of the elastic in place (or together). Even out the folds in the gathers formed by the elastic.

SHIRRING ELASTIC

Shirring is a method of gathering fabric using thin round elastic. Shirring elastic can be purchased, by the reel, in a variety of colours.

Before swing needle (zig-zag) machines were invented, shirring elastic was wound on the bobbin, either by machine, or by hand. This was a very hit and miss arrangement because it was difficult to gauge how tightly to wind the elastic on the bobbin.

Now the process is very different. The bobbin and top of the machine are threaded, in the normal way, with sewing thread. The shirring elastic is laid, in rows, on the wrong side of the fabric and stitched across with zig-zag stitch.

If you have a zig-zag foot which has a groove in the centre of the underside, use this foot; or if you have a braiding or cording foot which will guide the elastic down the centre of the foot, use this instead.

Method – To attach shirring elastic

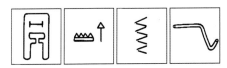

1 Set the machine as shown.

N O T E :

Remember to leave an opening in the casing to thread the elastic through!

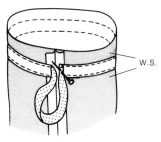

W.S.

Fig. 48 *Flat elastic is threaded into a straight stitched casing*

N O T E :

If your pattern has elastic round the sleeves always have the elastic slightly loose – it is very uncomfortable to have tight elastic, especially for children.

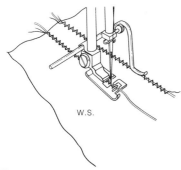

Fig. 49 *Stitch the elastic in place using the quilting guide to keep the rows parallel*

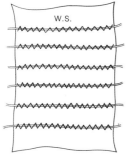

Fig. 50 *Stitch all the necessary rows of elastic in place*

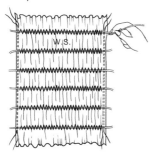

Fig. 51 *Stitch two rows of straight stitching down one side of the fabric to anchor the elastic. Pull into gathers. Stitch along the opposite side of the fabric to hold the elastic in place*

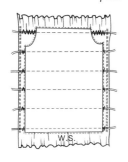

2 Set the distance between the quilting guide and the needle, to correspond with the distance required between the rows of elastic.

3 Pin the first row of elastic in place on the wrong side of the fabric along the right hand edge – there is no need to mark parallel lines on the fabric. Providing your first row of stitched elastic is straight, all subsequent rows will be straight, and the distance between them equal. The elastic is not stretched at this stage.

4 Stitch the elastic in place using a narrow zig-zag stitch which just *clears* the elastic.

5 The first row already stitched is moved to the right and fed under the quilting guide. The second row to be stitched is fed under the foot – you thereby ensure that it lays parallel to the first row (*fig. 49*). The distance between the two rows is set by the quilting guide. Keep your eye on the quilting guide whilst sewing.

6 Stitch all the necessary rows of elastic in place (*fig. 50*), moving each newly-stitched row to the right and feeding it under the quilting guide.

7 When all rows have been stitched, sew a couple of rows of straight stitching across one end of the fabric anchoring down the loose ends of elastic, or tie off the loose ends of elastic on one side.

8 Pull up the free ends of the elastic in pairs until the fabric is the required size (*fig. 51*).

9 Stitch or tie off the ends. The shirring is now complete – easy!

The advantages of this method are:

• The fabric remains flat whilst stitching is in progress.

• The lines for the elastic do not need to be marked on the fabric.

• You are in control of the finished size.

The finer the fabric the more fullness can be gathered with shirring elastic.

To cut out a pattern shape from shirred fabric, mark or tack round the shape, then machine one or two rows of tiny straight stitches around the shape (*fig. 52*). Cut out the shape just beyond the stitched line.

Fig. 52 *Mark the pattern shape on the shirred fabric, stitch on the marked line then cut out the shape*

EMBROIDERY (FREE)

FRAMING THE FABRIC

Most machine embroidery is worked in an embroidery hoop (not too large because it will hit the side of your machine: 20–25 cm (8–10 in) is a practical size to use). Lay the fabric right side uppermost over the larger ring of the frame and push the smaller ring inside. The right side of the fabric is then lying in the well of the frame (the opposite way from hand embroidery). You must stretch the fabric tightly in the frame before tightening up the screw (*fig. 53*).

You will find it easier to sew on small pieces of fabric so if a large project is planned it may be more practical to sew it in small sections and assemble them after the embroidery is completed.

Always have a spare hoop of fabric available to try stitches on before committing yourself to your embroidery.

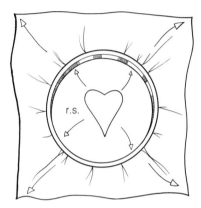

Fig. 53 *The right side of the fabric lies in the well of the hoop and is pulled taut*

PREPARING THE SEWING MACHINE

Make sure the bobbin area is oiled and free from fluff and cottons. Remove or cover the feed teeth, and remove the foot (and in some cases the leg and screw) as applicable.

Check your needle is straight and sharp. A good size to start with is 90 (14) but this will depend on the fabric used. Take note of your tension for normal sewing, then you can easily turn back when the embroidery is finished.

If your machine has a removable bobbin case it is a good idea to have a spare one to use for machine embroidery. Put a spot of nail varnish on this one then it will be readily identified. When you have finished the embroidery you can then change back to the other case and your bobbin tension will be ready for normal sewing.

On some machines you may have to bring the bobbin thread up through the fabric in the frame and hold both threads as you start to sew.

FREE EMBROIDERY STITCHING TECHNIQUES

Straight stitching

1 Set the machine as shown.

2 Do not forget to put the pressure foot lever down.

3 Try free-hand stitching. The more you move the frame the longer the stitch. Relax, breathe freely and get into a rhythm.

4 A speckled effect can be achieved by using a contrast colour on the bobbin and slightly increasing the top tension.

5 Try sewing the shapes in *fig. 54*.

Fig. 54 *Try free machining using straight stitch*

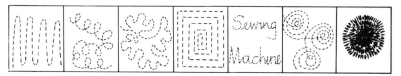

Zig-Zag stitching

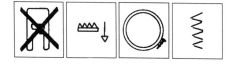

1 Set the machine as shown.

2 Lower the pressure foot lever.

3 Practice sewing with this stitch. You may like to vary the width control as you sew.

4 Try the shapes in *fig. 55*.

Fig. 55 *Practise sewing using zig-zag stitch*

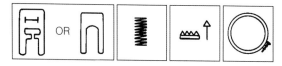

Satin stitch

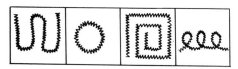

1 Set the machine as shown.

2 Sew with the stitching moving freely forward (without pushing or pulling the hoop). The stitches should lie touching each other in

a smooth continual line. Try moving the stitch width lever as you sew.

3 Practice straight lines and curves. If the stitching bunches forming a lump, you are 'holding on' to the hoop or the stitch length is too close to 0.

4 Try tapering to a point, e.g. when outlining a leaf (*fig. 56*).

Couching thread

Suitable threads for couching include knitting yarns e.g. chenille, mohair, wool (1-ply up to chunky weight), metallic threads, cords and string. You can use a cording foot or guide when couching – this helps to guide the threads (*fig. 57*).

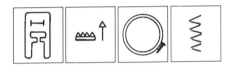

1 Set machine as shown.

2 Lay the couching threads on top of the fabric – hold them down or pin in place.

3 Stitch the couching threads to the fabric (*fig. 58*). Try straight and curved lines, and thin and thick couching threads.

4 The pressure control may need to be reduced when sewing down thick threads.

Twin needle sewing

A twin needle may be used when embroidering (for instructions see under Twin Needles, p. 105). Always remember when using a twin needle, the width control must never be set beyond half way, and the needle position should be central.

Wrapping threads

1 Set machine as shown. No fabric is needed for this.

2 Lower the pressure foot and sew over the cord, keeping it taut between your left and right hand whilst stitching (*fig. 59*).

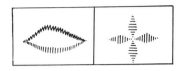

Fig. 56 *Shapes sewn using satin stitch*

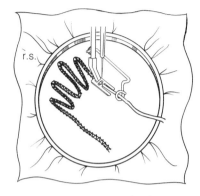

Fig. 57 *Couching a thread using a cording guide*

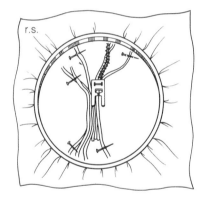

Fig. 58 *Couching threads using zig-zag stitch*

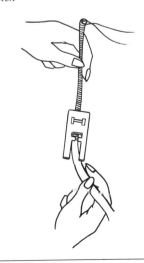

Fig. 59 *Wrapping a thread*

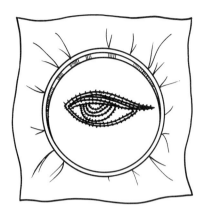

Fig. 60 *Whip stitch*

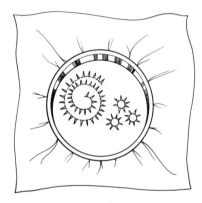

Fig. 61 *Feather stitch*

Whip stitch

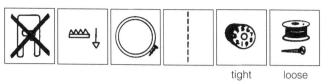

tight   loose

1 Set the machine as shown.

2 This is a textured versatile stitch. The top thread lies on the surface of the fabric and the loops from the bobbin thread come to the surface and cover the top thread making a corded solid line (*fig. 60*). Run the machine fast when sewing this stitch.

3 Try sewing this stitch in all directions and use it as a filling stitch.

Feather stitch

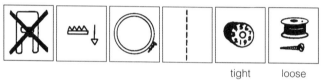

tight   loose

1 Set the machine as shown.

2 Although this stitch looks like zig-zag it is straight stitch sewn slowly in whirls and circles (*fig. 61*).

Free cable stitch

This stitch is used for sewing with threads which are too thick or textured to thread on the top of the machine, e.g. crochet cotton or bouclé.

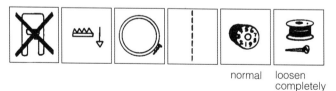

normal   loosen completely

Set the machine as shown. The embroidery is framed with the right side down on the bed of the machine (you will be sewing up side down from the wrong side). This stitch produces raised loose bobbly threads on the surface of the work. Thick smooth threads, e.g. crochet cotton, are wound onto the bobbin and may go through the tension spring on the bobbin. You can also use thicker threads and threads with loops and slubs, but they need to be wound manually onto the bobbin and must by-pass the bobbin tension spring.

N O T E :

Remember to lower the pressure foot lever!

Space stitching

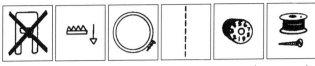

normal   normal

1 Set the machine as shown.

2 Draw circles on your framed fabric 3–4 cm (1–1½ in) across. Cut them out and stitch them one at a time (*fig. 62*).

3 Stitch across the space backwards and forwards keeping the stitches under tension (taut) and just catching the fabric round the edge of the circle (*fig. 62*). This method can also be worked across small squares.

4 You may wish to satin stitch around the cut edge when straight stitching is finished (*fig. 62*).

5 You can stitch this on spare fabric, stitching across the cut out circles fairly heavily. Then cut out the stitched portion (*fig. 63*) and use as flowers to sew down on an embroidery (*fig. 64*).

FREE EMBROIDERY – SPECIAL EFFECTS

Two threads in the needle

When sewing tree bark, for example, a good effect can be achieved by using two different colour threads through the eye of the needle. (The top tension may need to be set on a lower number).

Layering (reverse appliqué see under Appliqué, p. 9)

Fabric or net can be layered onto your base fabric and then satin stitch shapes can be worked. Some of the layers can then be cut away revealing different colours.

Machine embroidery needs patience, and much experimenting with stitches and different threads is needed (quite often the results are not always as planned!).

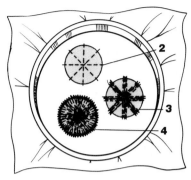

Fig. 62 *Space stitching*

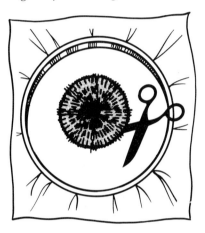

Fig. 63 *Cutting out the stitched flower*

Fig. 64 *A space stitched flower*

NOTE:

Keep your fingers on your hoop. It is not easy to see where the needle will enter the fabric.

COMMON FAULTS ENCOUNTERED
WHILST SEWING MACHINE EMBROIDERY

 Faults

 *Remedies*

Faults	Remedies
Needle doesn't pick up bobbin thread	Fabric needs tightening in the frame or needle needs replacing. Keep frame on bed of machine or try using a darning foot
'Birds nesting' Thread bunches on the back of the emboidery	Bring bobbin thread to the top of work when starting to sew and hold. Check top threading up
Bobbin area becomes jammed with thread	Pressure foot lever is not down when sewing. Always turn the balance wheel downwards and towards you when bringing the needle out of the fabric
Thread frays or breaks	Loosen top tension, sew smoothly – if fine or metallic thread is being used sew slower. Try a larger needle (it will have a bigger eye)
Loops on back of work, and jamming	Top thread needs re-threading
Needle breaks	Pulling or pushing the work and sewing too slowly

EMBROIDERY
(PRE-SET STITCHES)

If you like machine-embroidered garments and soft furnishings, but do not wish to design and sew your own patterns as in free embroidery, a machine which has a good selection of pre-set embroidery stitches is a must for you. Besides a selection of utility stitches many machines have a variety of outline patterns and block patterns (e.g. patterns made up of satin stitches). Machine embroidery is neater and the fabric lies flatter, especially when fine fabric is being stitched, if a length of stitch and tear vilene or even 'till roll' is laid beneath the fabric prior to stitching. Tear this from the back of the fabric when stitching has been completed. A wing needle used with open embroidery stitches gives an effect similar to drawn thread work. The machine embroidery patterns on older machines needed a lot of adjustment, but modern machines sew the patterns at the touch of a button. Computerized machines will also link patterns together, e.g. a stem, then a leaf, then a flower. On some, over fifty different patterns or letters can be linked together – great for name tapes! These can then be memorized and recalled days later. On some models the patterns can be mirror-imaged. This is particularly useful for sewing a design where the motif needs to face in different directions. Some machines have the facility to elongate patterns without changing the density of the stitch, e.g. a small scallop can be elongated to saucer size.

The latest development, and by far the most impressive, is the facility on such machines as New Home (Janome) Memory Craft 8000 to sew large multi-coloured satin stitch designs up to 70 × 125 cm (2¾ × 5 in) in size and using up to five different colours in a single motif. This was previously only possible on very expensive industrial machines.

The design is programmed into the machine by the use of memory cards. Each card contains numerous designs and several cards have been produced to date. It is easy to update the designs because new cards will be available periodically.

Once the design and colours have been chosen the fabric is put in a hoop and the start button is pressed (no foot control is necessary). You can sit back and have a cup of coffee, or read a book, since even the fabric does not need guiding through the machine! The machine stops automatically if the thread breaks or when a colour needs changing and at the end of a program.

If you wish to take this facility a step further an 'add-on' has been produced which can be likened to the scanners we are familiar with, which scan bar codes at supermarket check-outs.

This 'scan and sew' facility enables you to draw your own motif which is then scanned, in just a few seconds, onto a memory card. The card is then simply inserted into the sewing machine in the same manner as the pre-programmed cards.

You can choose to sew your design in up to four different colours and it can be up to 6 cm (2½ in) square, but of course if you require larger motifs they can easily be linked together. If you do not wish to draw your own designs, a photograph or drawing in a magazine or book can just as easily be scanned and an accurate copy will be transferred to your sewing.

There is so much scope with this facility, it is easy to become totally absorbed and fascinated. Do not be put off by terms such as 'scanning' and 'programming the machine', the equipment is very simple to use, and you do not need a degree to master it! If you enjoy creativity and like your clothes and soft furnishings to be completely unique, then this is a must for you.

FAULTS

Most simple faults are not due to the machine malfunctioning but are mainly caused by the operator, and can easily be rectified. If your machine is not stitching well (this always seems to happen when we are in a hurry!) do not panic. *Do not* reach for the tension dial – sudden poor stitching is very rarely due to the tension. Stay calm, re-thread the top thread, rewind the bobbin and change the needle. Check for fluff and scraps of cotton in the bobbin area. Nine times out of ten this is all that is required and the machine will stitch perfectly.

If, however, the fault persists check with the faults table below. If you are unable to rectify the fault after checking the table, seek professional help.

Symptoms	 Causes	Remedies
'Birds nesting', e.g. looping on the back of the fabric and down in the bobbin area	Machine incorrectly threaded	Rethread the machine
	Take-up lever not down	Lower the take-up lever before sewing
	Insufficient pressure on the foot	Check pressure control
	Balance wheel turned clockwise	Always turn the balance wheel anti-clockwise
	Bobbin thread not brought to the top after re-threading	Bring bobbin thread to the top before sewing
Fabric is pushed down through the needle plate into the bobbin area	Fabric is fine	For straight stitching change to the straight stitch foot and needle plate
	Needle is blunt	Fit a new needle
Fabric not moving forward	Feed teeth down	Raise feed teeth
	Pressure too loose	Increase pressure
	Stitch length set at 0	Check stitch length

Symptoms	Causes	Remedies
Fabric not moving forward (continued)	Stitching has bunched forming a lump	Increase stitch length
Foot pedal heats up	Resting foot on foot pedal whilst not actually sewing	Remove foot from pedal between sewing
Machine fails to operate	Switches not turned on	Check switches
	Fuse in the plug may need replacing	Check fuse in plug
	Electricity may have been turned off	Check to see if other electrical appliances are working
Machine jamming and knocking	Thread or a broken needle caught in the raceway	Clean out bobbin area (gentle vacuuming may be used)
Missed or irregular stitches	Blunt or bent needle	Change the needle
	Needle put in the wrong way round	Check the needle (if necessary consult your manual)
	Insufficient pressure on pressure foot	Increase the pressure
	Weights of thread not balanced	Balance the thicknesses of threads used
Missed stitches occurring on synthetic stretch fabrics	The needle is bouncing off the fabric	Try changing to a right or left needle position when sewing straight stitches
		Check that you are using a ball point needle of the correct thickness to suit the fabric
Needle breaks	Incorrect foot fitted	Check foot
	Incorrect needle plate for stitch	Check needle plate
	Work pushed or pulled through machine	Allow work to feed through at its own pace
	Needle inserted the wrong way round	Refit the needle
Puckering	Stitch length too long for thickness of fabric	Change to a shorter stitch length
	Zig-zag too wide for thickness of fabric	Change to a narrower stitch width
	Weights of thread not matched	Match weights of threads

Symptoms	Causes	Remedies
Stitches bunch at the start of sewing	Starting to sew too quickly Irregular pressure on the foot control	Start sewing smoothly. Hold the threads taut at the back of the foot when starting to sew
	Top thread may be caught on the cotton reel	Check cotton reel
	Not allowing the fabric to feed freely under the foot	Do not 'hold-on' to the fabric
Threads break	Using poor quality thread	Use a recommended thread
	Starting sewing with a jerk	Start off smoothly
	Burrs and scratches on the needle plate and raceway	Check needle plate and raceway – if rough, smooth off with a file or replace
	Thread catches on the cotton reel	Check cotton reel
	Thread wraps round the spool holder	Check spool holder
	Eye of the needle is rough	Check needle and change if necessary
	Weights of thread not matched	Use the same weights of thread
Threads not locking in the centre of the fabric	Weights (thicknesses) of the two threads not balanced	Use the same weights (thickness) of thread on the top and the bobbin
	Top and bottom tensions not correctly balanced	Reset tensions (see under Tensions, p. 94)

N O T E :

If the light on your machine fails, it does not always need replacing. The vibration from fast sewing can sometimes loosen the bulb, especially if it is a screw-in type. So test to see if it has worked loose before replacing.

FEET

See the pictures below for the feet that have been used in this book. The shape of the feet may vary slightly with different makes of machines.

NOTE:

Usually the feet marked * will come with the machine, but others need to be purchased separately.

Fig. 68 *Bias binding foot showing the binding funnel*

Fig. 69 *Blind hem foot**

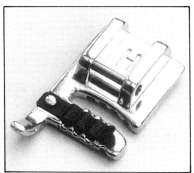

Fig. 70 *Braiding foot*

Fig. 71 *Button foot**

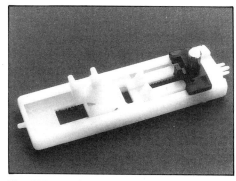

Fig. 72 *Buttonhole foot**

Fig. 73 *Darning foot*

Fig. 74 *Gathering foot*

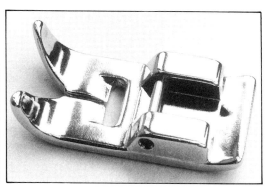

Fig. 75 *General purpose or zig-zag foot**

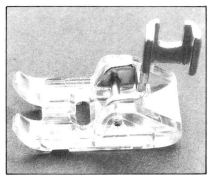
Fig. 76 *Plastic zig-zag foot**

Fig. 77 *Pleater*

Fig. 78 *Rolled hem foot**

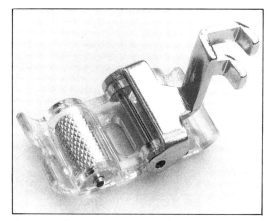
Fig. 79 *Roller foot*

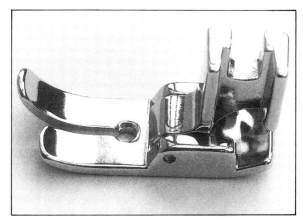
Fig. 80 *Straight stitch foot**

Fig. 81 *Walking foot*

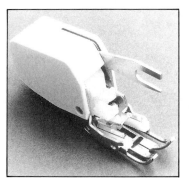

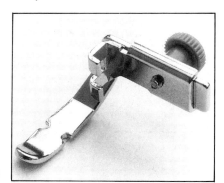
Fig. 82 *Zip foot**

Machine feet often fall into three categories, low bar, high bar or with clip on feet fitting: a low bar foot has a short leg between the foot and the screw and a high bar foot has a longer leg between the foot and the screw. If you are not sure whether your machine takes a high or a low bar fitting take a foot along with you when purchasing additional feet. A clip on foot just simply clips on to the bottom of the log. Two other very useful feet are:

Cording foot – this foot has a central groove on the underside, or a hole in the front of the foot, to guide the cord and varies with make.

Stretch stitch foot – this foot resembles a general purpose zig-zag foot, but has a raised bar running down the centre of the foot.

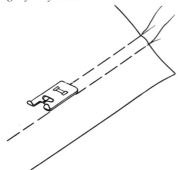

Fig. 83 *Use the quilting guide to keep the stitching straight and parallel to the edge of the fabric.*

Fig. 84 *Sew the parallel lines of stitching using the edge of the foot as a guide*

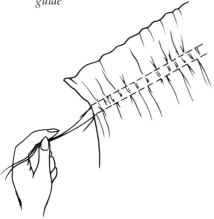

Fig. 85 *Gather the fabric by pulling the two bobbin threads simultaneously*

GATHERING

Method 1 – Gathering by sewing two parallel lines of long straight stitching

The finer the fabric, the fuller the gathers can be. Allow at least one and a half times the finished width. When gathering a long length of fabric, e.g. a frill round the bottom of a skirt or a frill round a cushion, it is advisable to divide the fabric to be gathered into quarters, and mark with pins. Also divide the skirt or cushion into quarters and mark. The fullness of the gathers will then be equally divided if you match the pins when sewing on the gathered frill.

1 Set the machine as shown, on the longest stitch length.

2 If you are gathering close to the edge of the fabric you may choose to line up the cut edge with the quilting guide. Your gathering stitching will then be exactly parallel to the edge of the fabric (*fig. 83*).

3 Sew two parallel lines of stitching. The second line can be sewn with the edge of the foot touching the first line of stitching (*fig. 84*).

4 Gather the fabric to the required length by pulling the two bobbin threads simultaneously (*fig. 85*). Spread the gathers evenly along the fabric. If you hold the top and bottom of the gathered fabric and give a tug the gathers will lie neatly.

5 To stitch the gathered frill to the main fabric put right sides together matching pins or marks and stitch in place from the gathered side. Sewing between the two lines of gathering thread. (Do not forget to change to a shorter stitch length).

6 Remove the gathering threads.

Cord Gathering

Cord gathering is used to gather thick or stiff fabrics, or in any situation when the two parallel rows of threads sewn for normal gathering are likely to break when they are pulled up to form the gathers. The principle is the same as for ribbon gathering. A strong cord, e.g. crochet cotton or button thread, is laid along the gathering line and a narrow zig-zag stitch is sewn over the cord. The stitching must be wide enough to clear the cord so it can be pulled up to form the gathers. A cording foot will help to feed the cord along the gathering line whilst sewing is in progress.

Method 2 – Gathering by using a double needle

It is possible to sew the two rows of long straight stitching simultaneously by using a double needle.

The drawback to this is that even when using a double needle with the widest distance between the needles, it does not give much space to sew the final row of stitching. This method, therefore, can only be used satisfactorily on fine fabrics. Also, because when using a double needle there is only one bobbin thread, the gathers would have to be pulled up by pulling the two top threads.

Method 3 – Ribbon gathering

This method of gathering is both decorative and practical and is a great favourite with me. It is especially useful for childrens' clothes because it can easily be adjusted on a finished garment. Some suggestions for uses are:

- Gathering cuffs or puffed sleeves
- Gathering the neck edge of a bonnet
- Gathering the waist of a child's dress
- Gathering the shoulder line on a sun dress
- Making a decorative two sided ruffle

Ribbon gathering is suitable for all fabrics but needs very narrow ribbon. The width of your zig-zag stitch needs to clear the width of the ribbon.

NOTE (method 1):

Do not try to achieve a short cut by only stitching one row of gathering thread, as this does not give a neat finish.

NOTE (method 3):

The stitch used is stretch zig-zag stitch, because of its strength (each stitch comprises three strands of thread). If you do not have stretch stitches on your machine you can use a zig-zag stitch, but you will need to thread the top of your machine with two threads. Bring them down through all the settings as if they were a single thread and pass both through the eye of the needle. Stitch a test run, and if the bobbin thread is showing on the top of your fabric slacken off the top tension, e.g. set on a lower number. Make a note of the original setting so you can easily put it back when you have finished.

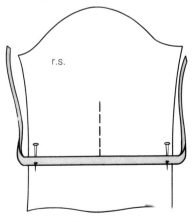

Fig. 86 *Mark the centre position and pin the ribbon in place*

1 Set the machine as shown. Make sure the stretch zig-zag stitch is set wide enough to clear your ribbon.

2 If you are gathering close to the edge of the fabric e.g. at the edge of a cuff you may like to line up the edge of the cuff with the quilting guide. Once you have set the desired width the ribbon will be sewn on parallel to the edge of the fabric. In most cases the ribbon is sewn on before the garment is made up and it is always sewn on to the right side of the fabric. I will use a cuff as an example.

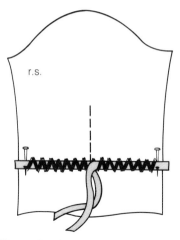

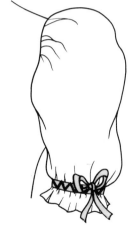

Fig. 87 *Stitch across the ribbon making sure that the stitches clear the edges of the ribbon. Pull the excess ribbon out at the centre to form the bow.*

Fig. 88 *Make up the garment and pull up the ribbon to form gathers, tie in a bow*

NOTE:

When using a pleater, because of its size, it is not always easy to see if the take-up lever is down and the foot is lowered ready for sewing. Always check before starting to sew.

Fig. 89 *A simplified drawing of a pleating foot showing the relevant parts*

3 Mark where the gathers are to be and pin a strip of narrow ribbon across the sleeve. Leave enough ribbon hanging from one side to tie a bow. Mark the centre of the sleeve (see *fig. 86* on p. 49).

4 Zig-zag across the ribbon. Make sure your stitching easily clears the ribbon.

5 When the stitching is completed pull out a loop of ribbon at the centre point using up the excess ribbon allowed for the bow (*fig. 87*). Cut through the centre of the loop.

6 The ends of the ribbon will be secured in the sleeve seam. Finish the cuff edge. Pull up the ribbon and tie a bow (*fig. 88*).

Gathering foot

Many machines have a special gathering foot as an optional extra. This foot gathers as it sews. Some feet will actually gather, and attach the gathered fabric to the main fabric in one operation. This is useful for gathering and applying lace. The only drawbacks are that the gathers are not very full. Only a minimal amount of fullness is used and it is difficult to estimate how much material, or lace, will be used in the gathers.

USING A PLEATER

A ruffler or pleater can be used on most machines (*fig. 89* shows how a pleater will fit on your machine). This is a very off-putting foot because it looks large and complicated. It is actually quite simple to use and gives a wonderfully neat row of very tiny pleats. I purchased a pleater years ago when I had to make dozens of ribbon rosettes and I have been delighted with it ever since.

The number of stitches between pleats can be adjusted, e.g. some pleaters will have three or more settings – one pleat every stitch, one pleat every sixth stitch, or one pleat every twelfth stitch.

The distance between the pleats can also be adjusted by lengthening or shortening the straight stitch length. The pleats are so small the appearance can look like incredibly neat gathers. Again, it is difficult to estimate the initial length of fabric required.

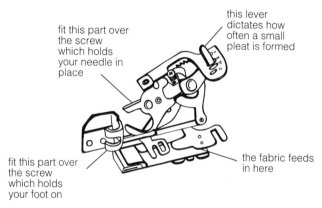

this lever dictates how often a small pleat is formed

fit this part over the screw which holds your needle in place

fit this part over the screw which holds your foot on

the fabric feeds in here

HEMS

There are many ways of finishing a hem. The method chosen will depend on the type of fabric being used and the purpose of the hem:

• Straight hems are generally worked along the straight of grain and are the easiest to sew

• Flared hems will require the extra fullness pinned into small pleats (or gathered) before sewing

• Very narrow rolled hems are only used on thin or sheer fabrics and should not be pressed

• Bias hems (e.g. circular skirts) should be allowed to hang before stitching and only very narrow hems are worked

The hem is usually the last finishing stage to a garment. Some hems are only turned up once, e.g. hems made on stretch fabrics or hems sewn on bulky fabrics. Hems can also be made using flat tape, or in some cases where only a very light hem is required, lace may be used. Fabrics which fray easily are turned over twice.

SEWING A BLIND HEM

Method 1 – Turning up a double hem

The secret of success when making a blind hem is to practice on a scrap of fabric first (it must be the same fabric that you will be using). The long stitch must just catch the top fabric, and the foot or stitch width may need adjustment. You must use a blind hem foot, though the style and shape of blind hem feet varies with the make of machine so consult your manual. If your machine does not have a blind hem stitch you can hem using a zig-zag on a long stitch length. Here the left hand point of the zig-zag stitch must just catch the top fabric. The way the hem is folded for sewing is of prime importance, so follow the diagrams carefully.

On a well executed blind hem the stitches on the right side will be practically invisible!

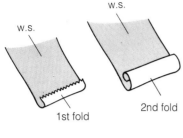

1st fold

2nd fold

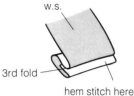

3rd fold

hem stitch here

Fig. 90 *Folding sequence for blind hemming, when turning up a double hem*

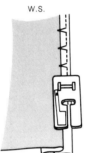

Fig. 91 *Stitching a double folded blind hem*

Fig. 92 *Folding sequence for blind hemming for a single folded hem*

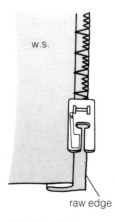

raw edge

Fig. 93 *A single folded hem being neatened and stitched simultaneously*

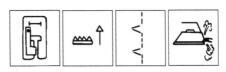

1 Set the machine as shown.

2 Fold the hem as described below and as shown in *fig. 90*.
1st fold - Fold the raw edge over onto the wrong side of the fabric.
2nd fold - Fold over again to enclose the raw edge. Turn the main fabric away from the hem making a:
3rd fold - And exposing a small border on the fabric inside the first fold. This is where the stitching will be, along the inside of the first fold.

Look carefully at the diagrams. Once the hem is folded correctly and the stitch setting is correct a perfect hem can be achieved with ease.

3 Stitch the hem in place (*fig. 91*). Then open out the third fold.

Method 2 – Turning up a single hem

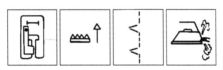

This method follows the same instructions as for a double hem but the stitch used neatens the edge of the fabric and hems at the same time. Also, the second fold is omitted (*figs. 92-93*).

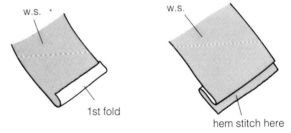

1st fold

hem stitch here

SEWING A DECORATIVE STRAIGHT HEM

This double hem is sewn first with straight stitch and then stitched again using a line of satin stitch. The satin stitch adds weight to the hem and it can look very effective when used on table linen.

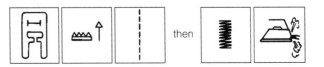

then

1 Set the machine as shown using straight stitch first.

2 Turn up a double hem and straight stitch in place (*fig. 94*).

3 Change the stitch setting to satin stitch (see under Stitches, p. 91).

4 Sew a row of satin stitch directly on top of the line of straight stitching (*fig. 95*). A machine embroidery thread gives a silky finish and makes a good contrast when sewn on linen.

A simple straight hem

Follow method three but omit the satin stitch.

SEWING A HEM USING LACE

This type of hem is edged along the inside with soft narrow lace. It creates a hem with a touch of luxury on delicate or fine fabrics.

1 Set the machine as shown.

2 Press up a single narrow hem (*fig. 96*), then open it out.

3 Pin the lace in place along the narrow hem on the right side of the fabric with the top edge of the lace against the pressed fold.

4 Straight stitch in place (*fig. 97*). Remember to reduce your stitch length if using a fine fabric.

5 Fold up the hem and catch the lace in place by hand (*fig. 98*).

SEWING A LETTUCE HEM

This type of hem is most successful when worked on knitted or stretch fabrics. It produces a decorative, fluted hem. This looks very attractive when sewn as a hem for a flared skirt.

Method

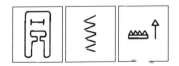

1 Set the machine as shown.

2 Fold under the single hem allowance (only a very narrow hem is needed 0.5 cm) (¼ in).

3 Sew a narrow zig-zag stitch over the folded edge, stretching the

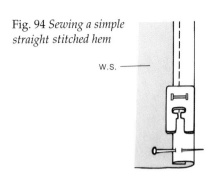

Fig. 94 *Sewing a simple straight stitched hem*

w.s.

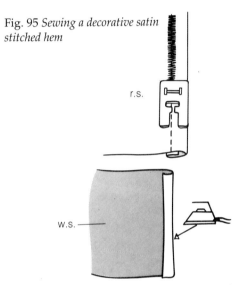

Fig. 95 *Sewing a decorative satin stitched hem*

r.s.

w.s.

Fig. 96 *Press up a single narrow hem*

Fig. 97 *Open out the pressed fold and straight stitch the lace on the right side. The top of the lace lies against the pressed fold*

r.s.

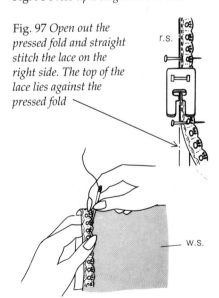

w.s.

Fig. 98 *Turn up the hem and sew in place by hand*

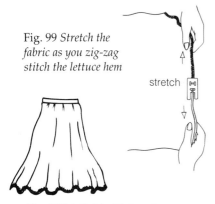

Fig. 99 *Stretch the fabric as you zig-zag stitch the lettuce hem*

stretch

Fig. 100 *A finished lettuce hem*

Fig. 101 *Pin the rick-rack braid over the folded hem ready for sewing*

Fig. 102 *As seen from the right side with only half of the braid protruding below the hem line*

Fig. 103 *Stitch the braid in place*

fabric as much as possible as you sew (*fig. 99*). You will need to keep stopping to adjust your hands.

4 Trim away any excess fabric from the back of the hem.

SEWING A RICK-RACK HEM

I am not normally fond of rick-rack braid but there are instances where it can look attractive. A decorative straight hem can be made using rick-rack braid.

Method

1 Set the machine as shown.

2 Turn up a narrow hem and press in place.

3 Lay a strip of rick-rack braid under the hem with only half of the braid protruding below the hem. Pin if necessary (*figs. 101-102*).

4 Stitch in place from either the right or wrong side (*fig. 103*).

SEWING A ROLLED HEM

This method of hemming requires a little practice just to become familiar with the way the foot works. A rolled hem is a very narrow, unpressed hem only suitable for use on fine fabrics.

Method

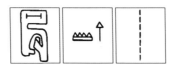

1 Set the machine as shown. It may be necessary to fit the straight stitch needleplate.

2 Turn up a tiny hem 2 mm (⅛ in) wide.

3 Feed the edge of the tiny hem down the scroll of the foot, draw it through, hold it in place with the point of the needle – lower the foot.

4 Whilst stitching take care when feeding the fabric through the foot. The fabric should automatically make a double fold as it passes along the scroll (see *fig. 104* on p. 55).

SEWING A SATIN STITCH SCALLOP HEM

A decorative hem can be sewn using satin stitch scallop stitch. This is particularly useful when hemming curves, e.g. a circular table cloth, or round a single thickness collar. (For instructions, see under Stitches, Scallop Stitch, p. 93).

SEWING A SHELL HEM

A shell hem is a decorative hem which can be used on stretch fabrics, light-weight woven fabrics, and fabrics which are cut on the bias. It can be used for edging straps, hems or frills. The top tension may need tightening depending on the fabric being used, so make a sample first. The longer the stitch length the larger the 'shell'.

Method

 tighten

1 Set the machine as shown.

2 Fold up a narrow single or double hem and press in place.

3 Sew along the edge of the fabric taking care to keep the long stitches beyond the folded edge (*fig. 105*).

SEWING A STRAIGHT STITCH SCALLOP HEM

This hem can be sewn on a folded hem or using a hem facing.

Method

1 Set the machine as shown

2 Fold the hem right sides together (or lay the facing along the hem, raw edges together, right sides facing).

3 Stitch the hem (*fig. 106*), using a pre-set straight stitch scallop, 1 cm (⅜ in) from the fold (or edge).

4 Trim close to the stitching and clip as shown (*fig. 107*).

5 Turn the hem to the wrong side and press.

6 If larger scallops are required a template should be used. The curves can be marked on the fabric using a water soluble pen.

Fig. 104 *Roll the hem between your right finger and thumb as it feeds into the foot*

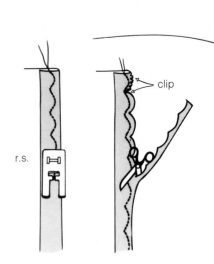

Fig. 105 *The long stitches must just clear the folded edge of the hem. (It may be necessary to tighten the top tension)*

Fig. 106 (Left) *With right sides together stitch the hem using a preset straight stitch scallop*
Fig. 107 (Right) *Trim close to the stitching line and clip as shown, before turning the hem to the wrong side*

r.s. clip

HOOPS

SEWING IN A HOOP

Hoops can be used when machining with the foot on or off. The reasons for sewing in a hoop are as follows:

- The fabric is kept taut and flat and is less likely to pucker if heavily stitched.

- The fabric is more manageable, and it is much easier to guide round shapes and small curves, for example.

- In order to machine with the foot off and the feed teeth lowered or covered, the fabric must be very taut and must be flat on the bed of the machine. This can be achieved by framing the fabric in a hoop. Also when the foot is off it is very difficult to know where the needle will enter the fabric so if you hold the edge of the hoop to guide the fabric your fingers will be out of harm's way.

FRAMING UP THE FABRIC

To sew in a hoop on the sewing machine the fabric to be stitched needs to lay in the well of the hoop, right side up. (For hand embroidery, it is the opposite way round.)

    The size of the hoop will depend on the distance between the needle and the upright on the right hand side of the machine, and also the size of the fabric you are working on. You may need to use a very tiny hoop, but do not forget, if you are sewing with the foot on, the foot will prevent you from sewing right up to the edge of the hoop.

To frame the fabric

1 Lay the larger ring on the work bench.

2 Lay the fabric right side uppermost over the larger ring. Centre your design.

3 Place the smaller ring on top of the fabric and inside the larger ring.

4 Push well down. Pull the outer fabric so that the fabric inside the hoop lays taut (*fig. 108*).

5 Tighten up the screw with a screwdriver, where applicable.

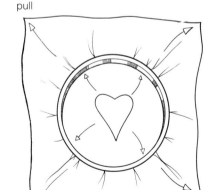

pull

pull

Fig. 108 *Lay the fabric right side uppermost over the larger ring. Centre the design and press the smaller ring inside the larger ring. Pull the fabric taut. Where applicable, tighten up the screw*

Most people already own a hoop which they use for hand embroidery. This is fine to use on the machine. A practical size is 20 cm (8 in) across. Larger hoops will hit the side of the machine and smaller ones will need moving frequently, unless only a very small area is to be stitched.

When sewing in a hoop with the foot on, hand embroidery hoops are sometimes too thick to slide under the foot of the machine. If this is the case, try to lift your take-up lever up another notch. (This is possible on some machines). If you are still unable to slide the hoop under the foot try lowering the feed teeth, but do not forget to raise them again when the hoop is in place.

If again the hoop still will not go under the foot, you will have to remove the foot each time. This can be a chore so you may decide to purchase a slim hoop which is sold especially for the sewing machine. This hoop consists of an outer plastic ring with a spring metal inner ring which is squeezed together with two handles to insert it into the plastic ring. However, I do not find this hoop as useful because it will not hold thick fabrics very well. When you are sewing in a hoop with the foot on you will need to be able to turn the material in all directions. To make this easier, the pressure on the foot may need reducing (see under Pressure Control, p. 75).

LACE

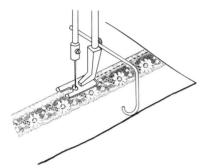

Fig. 109 *Sew the lace in place and keep parallel with the hem, or the edge of the fabric, by using the quilting guide*

There are several methods of attaching lace.

Method 1 – Attaching flat or pre-gathered lace

1 Set the machine as shown above.

2 Position the lace on the right side of the fabric and pin in place at intervals.

3 Set the required distance between the quilting guide and the needle. The quilting guide is used to keep the edge of the fabric parallel with the bottom of the lace. This is particularly helpful when applying a row of lace a short distance from a hem or cuff.

4 Feed the lace under the foot keeping the hem or the edge of the fabric in line with the quilting guide.

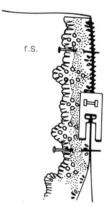

Fig. 110 *With the right sides facing zig-zag stitch the lace and the edge of the fabric together*

5 Sew in place using a straight or zig-zag stitch (a zig-zag stitch is often less noticeable) (*fig. 109*).

Method 2 – Attaching flat lace to a narrow hem

This technique neatens the fabric edge at the same time.

1 Set machine as shown above.

2 Lay the top of the lace level with the cut edge of the hem, right sides together.

3 Zig-zag the edges together (*fig. 110*).

4 Turn up a narrow hem and press.

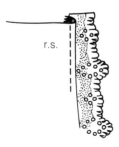

Fig. 111 *Turn up a narrow hem and stitch in place by hand or machine*

5 Stitch the hem in place by hand or machine (*fig. 111*).

Method 3 – Lace edged tucks

When sewing tucks (not pin tucks), you may like to have a lace edge showing below each tuck. This can look very attractive on christening gowns, cuffs or underwear.

1 Set the machine as shown.

2 Mark the fold and stitching lines on the fabric.

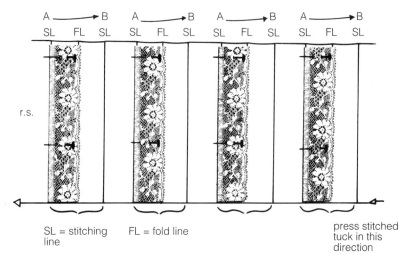

SL = stitching line   FL = fold line

press stitched tuck in this direction

Fig. 112 (Left) *Mark the stitching lines and fold lines on the fabric and pin the top of the lace in place along alternate stitching lines*

Fig. 113 (Below) *Press along each fold line and stitch the lace in place through all layers*

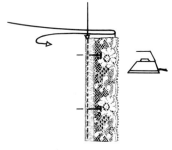

3 Use a lightweight flat lace. Lay the top of the lace, right side down, along alternate stitching lines on the right side of the marked fabric. (The lace will need to be wider than the tuck in order for it to show below it). Pin in place (*fig. 112*).

4 Stitch each tuck, (through the lace and double fabric), on the stitching line (*fig. 113*). Making sure the stitching is as near to the top of the lace as possible. (You may find it easier if you press the fold line in the centre of each tuck before stitching).

5 Press the tuck down. A narrow edge of lace will now show below the tuck.

6 Sew several rows of tucks and lace as described for a really fancy finish (*fig. 114*).

Fig. 114 *When several rows of tucks have been stitched, press them down so an edge of lace is visible beneath each tuck*

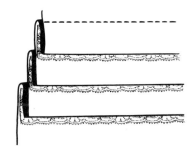

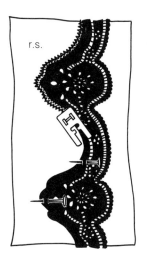

Fig. 115 *Zig-zag the lace to the right side of the fabric following the top curves of the lace*

Fig. 116 *On the wrong side, carefully cut away the excess fabric close to the zig-zag stitching*

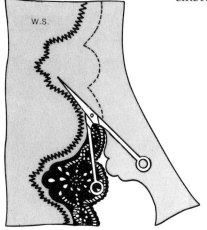

Method 4 – Attaching shaped lace

This method is used when attaching lace which has a shaped top. It is used on underwear, where sometimes the lace is cut into motifs and sewn on.

1 Set the machine as shown.

2 Position the lace on the garment with pins.

3 Sew the wrong side of the lace to the right side of the garment with zig-zag stitch following the top curves of the lace (*fig. 115*).

4 With small sharp scissors and the wrong side facing, carefully cut the fabric away behind the lace. Take care not to cut the lace. Do not cut too close to the zig-zag stitching (*fig. 116*).

Insertion lace can be sewn in this way if desired, but both edges of the lace are zig-zagged and the strip of fabric under the lace is cut away.

Lace can also be used to make a lightweight decorative hem. (For instructions see under Hems, p. 53.) You may also like to make your own Broderie anglaise lace (*fig. 117*) by using a scallop stitch and embroidery stitches (see under Stitches, Scallop Stitch, p. 93).

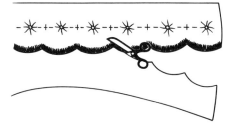

Fig. 117 *Make your own Broderie anglaise lace with scallop stitch and preset embroidery stitches*

Maintenance

Sewing machines need very little maintenance but they should be cleaned and, where applicable oiled regularly. Obviously, the more use your machine has, the more often it will need cleaning. Some fabrics create more fluff than others, so check the bobbin area for lint frequently.

CLEANING

The most important parts to be cleaned are the bobbin raceway, feed teeth and needle plate. Become familiar with the mechanism of your bobbin area: many modern, front loading bobbins have two knobs which push aside to release the raceway. I find this easier if the machine is tilted backwards onto a cushion. Always check the raceway when a needle has broken, because you *must* retrieve the broken tip of the needle. It can become lodged in the raceway and scratch it: this causes a roughened surface which can catch on the sewing thread and break or damage it.

Cleaning instructions

1 Disconnect the machine from the electricity supply.

2 Remove the needle plate and brush out all lint from the feed teeth.

3 If your machine has a front loading bobbin, lay the machine on its back (supported by a cushion).

4 Remove the bobbin case.

5 Remove the raceway where applicable. *Take care*: note which way round the parts are placed!

6 Brush out all fluff and lint. I sometimes vacuum this area with the end of a vacuum cleaner hose, especially if the machine has a top loading bobbin. If your vacuum cleaner has a method of controlling the power of the suction try a gentle approach first!

7 Wipe the cleaned area with a cotton wool bud with a little machine oil on it.

8 Before re-assembling the parts run your fingers over the parts removed from the raceway and the needle plate. Check for any scratches or roughened areas. If any are present try filing them with

a file or nail emery board to smooth out any roughness. If the scratches are too deep the parts will need replacing.

9 Re-assemble the parts and manually turn the balance wheel (get into the habit of always turning this wheel downwards and towards you) to check that you have re-assembled the parts correctly and that the needle is freely entering the bobbin area.

10 Wipe any accumulated fluff from the needle bar. Keep your machine covered when not in use.

OILING

It is difficult to generalize about oiling because some of the more recent machines (mainly the electronic and computerized models) do not require oiling. Therefore, you need to check your machine instruction book. Always use sewing machine oil, as most other oils are unsuitable: they are either too thick or they solidify and clog up the machine. If you use your machine frequently and are familiar with the way it sounds you will notice a harshening of the sound which indicates that the machine needs oiling. If you are putting your machine into store, or will not be using it for a long time, oil it before storing it away.

Most machines which require oiling have a series of holes, sometimes painted red, to indicate where oil is required. Some models need the top plate removed to adequately oil the machine.

Do not put too much oil in these holes, just one drop in each. Do not over oil.

To oil the machine (if applicable)

1 Switch off the power supply.

2 Drop one drop of oil into each appropriate hole.

3 Run the machine with out any thread or fabric in it for a few minutes to distribute the oil.

4 Wipe the outside surfaces of the machine with kitchen roll to absorb any excess oil.

5 Sew on a piece of cotton or calico (with the machine threaded up) to ensure all the surplus oil is absorbed and will not spoil your sewing.

If you follow these simple maintenance steps regularly your machine should give you years of trouble-free sewing.

NEEDLES

One often undervalued aspect of the sewing machine is the needle: changing can make a marked difference to the stitch quality, and in most cases it is not changed often enough. Needles must be changed to suit the weight and type of fabric being sewn. I like to compare machine needles with knitting needles: we would not knit chunky yarn on a thin needle yet we try to sew thick fabric without changing to a thicker needle, and vice versa. It may be because we are short of time, or perhaps just cannot be bothered. So lets change our habits and change our needles!

Needles can become blunt like pencils or bent, causing pulls and snags in the fabric, irregular stitching or missed stitches (*fig. 118*). This is caused because the needle is now not long enough to pick up the bobbin thread each time.

There are no real guide lines as to when to replace your needle because different fabrics react differently with the needle, some blunting it quicker than others, but a general rule would be to replace the needle after every two garments. You will soon learn to judge this for yourself. Become familiar with the way your needle fits into your machine. If it is put in the wrong way round the machine will not stitch properly, or the needle may break after hitting the foot or needle plate.

It is often difficult to see at a glance what size or type of needle you have on your machine. The writing on the needle is very hard to read even if you have good eyesight! Some manufacturers are now colour coding the head of the needle so the size can be identified at a glance. It is well worth looking out for these. Also choose a good quality needle, as cheap needles tend to blunt and bend more easily.

There are many types and sizes of needles available and this can sometimes be confusing. The needles I have listed overleaf are usually adequate for the average sewer.

Fig. 118 *An example of irregular stitching caused by a blunt, or bent needle*

NON-STRETCH (WOVEN) FABRICS

A standard needle is used for non-stretch fabrics. It has a sharp pointed tip and pierces through the fibres of the fabric. It comes in a variety of sizes (thicknesses).

Size of Needle	Fabric
60, 65, 70 (8, 9, 10)	These are very fine needles and are suitable for very lightweight fabrics: lace, net, organdy, lawn, fine silk, polyester and voile.
75, 80, 90 (11, 12, 14)	These needles are in the middle of the range and are suitable for the largest range of fabrics: cotton, medium weight wool, poplin, viscose, polycotton, linen, needlecord, twill and brocade.
100 (16)	This is a really strong needle and is used for: thick upholstery fabrics and canvas.

A 'jeans' or denim needle is also available and is a thick needle which is slightly longer; it has a sharper point which enables the needle to pass easily through thick, stiff fabrics such as denim.

STRETCH (KNITTED) FABRICS

A ball point needle is used to sew stretch fabrics. It has a rounded point, so instead of passing through the fibres it passes between them, thus eliminating the chance of 'runs' from the seams of the knitted fabric. Again, these needles come in various thicknesses and should be matched to the weight of the knitted fabric.

MORE SPECIALIZED NEEDLES

There are more specialized needles available, but these are sometimes difficult to locate. I find the most useful of these are the following:

Twin or double needle

This needle has one shank which pushes up into the machine and two needles which branch out from it (*fig. 119*). The gap between the two needles can vary. Its use is explained under Twin Needle Sewing (p. 107).

Fig. 119 *A double or twin needle*

Triple needle

This is the same as the twin needle but has one more needle joined to the top shank (*fig. 120*).

Leather needle

A leather needle has a wedge-shaped point to sew cleanly through leather or suede. It should never be used on fabric because it will cut through the fibres.

Fig. 120 *A triple needle*

Slotted or easythread needle

This needle is suitable for people who find needle threading difficult, or for the partially sighted (*fig. 121*). The needles come in most sizes except the finest. The needles look like standard needles but they have a slit at the top right hand side of the eye, so by sliding the thread down the right hand side of the needle, it slips through the slit into the eye and the needle is then threaded ready for sewing. When sewing is in progress, the tension of the thread in the eye of the needle is downwards and backwards, and thus the needle remains threaded.

Perfect stitch needle

This type of needle is used on fine synthetic fabrics and it helps to minimize skipped stitches.

Fig. 121 *An easy thread needle showing the slit which the thread slips into, on the top right hand side of the eye*

Top stitching needles

If you are top stitching with a thick thread and find threading your needle difficult, look out for special top stitching needles with large eyes.

Wing needles

A wing needle is usually only available in specialist sewing machine shops. It is a broad needle having wide flanges along either side. This type of needle makes a larger hole in the fabric and when used in conjunction with open embroidery stitches gives a very decorative appearance to the fabric. Good results can be obtained by using open stitches, e.g. honeycomb smocking stitch, in rows on lawn. (However, block stitches, e.g. embroidery stitches using satin stitch, are unsuitable). It is necessary to stabilize the fabric first, to stop it puckering, by laying 'stitch and tear vilene' or strips of 'till roll' or 'calculator roll' beneath the fabric before sewing commences. The backing is torn off after stitching is completed. Alternatively the fabric can be put into an embroidery hoop ready for stitching.

NOTE:

Not all makes of needle fit all machines. If in doubt, take one of your old needles with you when buying new ones.

OVERLOCKERS

The main purpose of an overlocker, a machine you may be unfamiliar with, is to neaten seams, the finished seam being similar to those found on garments in shops. The overlocker trims the seam as it sews, thus producing a very neat edge to the fabric. Overlockers have other functions and attachments, and on some makes the blades are retractable making the machine more versatile. They will sew a rolled hem second to none, they also sew a blind hem, gather and attach flat elastic.

Overlockers operate at much faster speeds than domestic sewing machines. If, for example, you were sewing flat elastic to the top of a waist slip, an overlocker would attach the elastic, gather the fabric and neaten the edge in one operation. However, it is not practical to have an overlocker instead of a sewing machine because it will not sew a straight stitch, make a buttonhole or insert a zip. An overlocker compliments a domestic sewing machine, it does not replace it. For people who mainly dressmake, it would be better to have a fairly basic, middle-of-the-range sewing machine and an overlocker rather than an expensive multifunctional sewing machine.

Overlockers can look complicated because there are so many reels of thread to thread up, but modern overlockers have colour coded charts on the machines to aid threading. Once the machine is threaded, changing a thread requires nothing more than cutting off the old thread close to the cone and knotting on a new one. The machine can then be run on an odd scrap of fabric until the new thread passes through all the settings, or on some models the threads can be pulled out from under the foot until the new thread appears. Overlockers do not have bobbins, as all the threads feed directly from the top spool holders. They fall into one of three categories:

Three-thread overlockers

A three-thread overlocker is self-explanatory. It has one thread which passes through the needle, a top looper thread which lies sideways on top of the fabric and a lower looper thread which lies sideways on the underside of the fabric.

The three-thread overlocker can be converted to use two threads, usually by just turning a knob. This is more economical when matching thread to fabric, as only two reels are used. The stitching on a three-thread overlocker looks like (*fig. 122*).

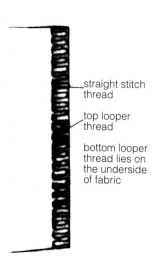

straight stitch thread

top looper thread

bottom looper thread lies on the underside of fabric

Fig. 122 *Stitching produced by a three-thread overlocker showing the row of straight stitches and the top looper stitches*

Four-thread overlockers

A four-thread overlocker sews with two needles so it sews two rows of straight stitching. It also has a top looper thread and a lower looper thread. For an example of the stitching see *fig. 123* .

One needle can be removed to convert the machine to a three-thread machine. If the right hand needle is removed a wide overlock is sewn with one row of straight stitching (*fig. 124a*). If the left hand needle is removed a narrower overlock is sewn with one row of straight stitching (*fig. 124b*).

A four-thread overlocker is very useful for seaming and overlocking in one operation. The seam is stronger since there are two rows of straight stitching.

Differential feed overlockers

A differential feed overlocker has been designed to cope well with fabrics which pucker or stretch. Two feed dogs are used: one feeds the fabric through the machine, and the other pushes or pulls the fabric to keep it flat whilst it is being stitched.

Most overlockers have the facility to sew a cord into the seam simultaneously as they seam and overlock. This is particularly useful when seaming stretch fabric, as the cord helps to stabilize the fabric. This can be used to advantage on shoulder seams where the seam is apt to stretch.

The only drawback to owning an overlocker is the large amount of thread that it consumes. This can be offset by purchasing large cones of cheaper thread especially produced for overlockers. It is not practical to have a wide colour range. If you have just purchased an overlocker you may start with the appropriate number of cones in just two shades – maybe black and white, or navy and cream. You can economize by buying smaller reels for the spools which feed the needle/needles. They use less thread than the loopers.

Once you have experienced using an overlocker you will never be satisfied with the seam finish on a domestic zig-zag machine!

Fig. 123 *Stitching produced by a four-thread overlocker showing two rows of straight stitching for extra strength, and the top looper stitches*

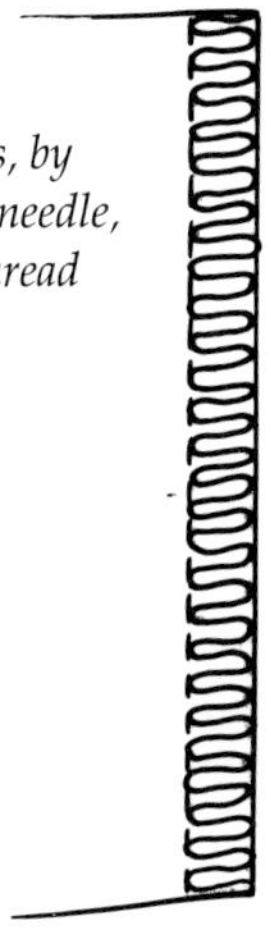

Fig. 124a *Four threads, converted to three threads, by removing the right-hand needle, producing a wide three thread overlocking stitch*

Fig. 124b *Four threads, converted to three threads, by removing the left-hand needle, producing a narrow three thread overlocking stitch*

PATCHWORK

The concept of patchwork has changed over the years. Initially it was a practical method of recycling used fabrics, but with time the craft has developed as a creative opportunity to express individual designs and shapes, best achieved with new fabrics. When sewing geometric shapes together accuracy in marking, cutting and sewing the fabric is essential.

COLOURS

Years ago there was not the choice of fabric or colour that there is today. Patchwork had to be made from the limited fabric available at the time. Now there is almost too much choice so care must be taken when choosing the colours to use. Lots of bright colours, haphazardly arranged, tend to make the patchwork garish and gaudy. (Remember in the old patchwork the colours of the fabrics used had already mellowed with time).

It is the colour and design which initially attracts us to a piece of patchwork, not the sewing expertise. If you want a subtle look, choose a few complimentary colours and stick to these throughout. This does not mean that you can only use a few fabrics. I like to use lots of different fabrics, some patterned, some plain, some textured, some smooth. Also vary the size of the patterns on the fabric. Stick to a few well chosen colours but vary the depth of these colours.

If you like a brighter, bolder look, still stick to a few colours but spice them up by adding a little of a dramatic colour, e.g. purple, bright pink, or turquoise.

FABRICS

Your fabric choice should depend on whether you intend to wash or dryclean the patchwork. If the patchwork is to be washed, choose easily laundered fabrics of similar weight, e.g. cotton, polycotton, dress weight or lightweight furnishing fabrics, etc. It may be necessary to wash the fabrics before use to avoid shrinkage later.

If the patchwork is to be drycleaned, the choice of fabric is much larger and a variety of different weights can be used in the same piece of work – e.g. silk, satin, velvet, wool or taffeta. Avoid stretch or knitted fabrics.

DESIGN

Many patchwork designs adapt well to being sewn on a sewing machine. Of the geometric designs, strips, squares, triangles and rectangles are the most easily managed. Crazy or Victorian patchwork, using random shapes, is quick and effective when sewn on the sewing machine. When making a large item in machine patchwork, you will find it easier to handle if you work it in small sections which you can sew together later. Bear this in mind when planning your design.

Try to draw your design first, and then lay out your fabrics balancing both the colours and the density of patterning on the fabrics. Crazy patchwork is designed as you pin the patches in place.

EASY MACHINE PATCHWORK

Instructions for working log cabin patchwork

Log cabin patchwork is made up of strips of fabric sewn onto a square of backing fabric. The first patch positioned in the middle of the square is usually bright and represents the fire in the centre of the cabin. The surrounding strips represent the logs forming the cabin. Traditionally, two sides are sewn using dark fabrics to represent the sides of the cabin in the shade, the other two sides using lighter fabrics to represent the two sides of the cabin in the sunlight. The colour is also graded outwards from the centre patch. You can join these finished squares together to form different patterns depending on how the dark and light sides are arranged. Experiment when you have sewn a few: you can make a cushion cover, for example, from one large square or from four smaller squares sewn together; or a quilt using numerous small squares sewn together.

NOTE:

Always cut your patches out on the straight of grain.

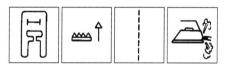

1 Set the machine as shown.

2 Having selected your fabrics, cut out long thin strips. I use a ruler and draw a line down each edge with a pencil or water soluble pen or you could use a rotary cutter and board.

3 Cut a foundation square from calico or sheeting. The size will depend on the size of the finished item. For a cushion measuring 40 cm (16 in) you will require four squares of foundation fabric each measuring 11.5 cm (4½ in). It is better to be over generous, you can always trim any excess off later.

Figs. 125-127 *Mark a diagonal cross on the backing fabric, pin and stitch the first patch in the centre with the corners touching the diagonal cross. It is essential to press open each patch as it is sewn*

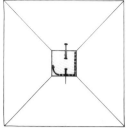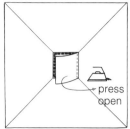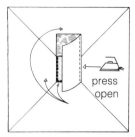

NOTE:

It is essential that each patch is pressed over before the next patch is sewn. (I keep a travel iron set up on the right hand side of the machine).

4 Mark a diagonal cross on the foundation fabric.

5 Pin the first square patch in place in the centre of the fabric. A good size to use is a square measuring the width of your ruler on all four sides. The corners of the square patch will touch the diagonal lines on the backing fabric. Sew in place close to the raw edge (*fig. 125*).

Fig. 128 *This is the sewing order, and the light and dark sequence of the patches*

6 Follow *figs. 126-128*, stitching two patches in each fabric, keeping two sides of the square dark and two sides light. It is important to have the same seam allowance on each patch, so line up the raw edges with the edge of the foot when sewing.

Brick patchwork

Another easy geometric shape to sew are oblongs arranged in a brick formation.

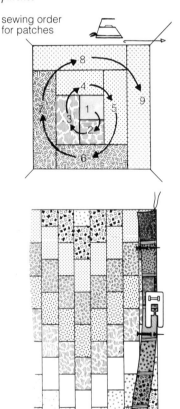

1 Set the machine as shown.

2 Mark and cut all the patches from the same template.

3 Sew long strips of patches by joining together the short edges of the oblongs (*fig. 129*). Use the edge of the foot as a seam guide.

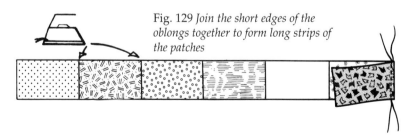

Fig. 129 *Join the short edges of the oblongs together to form long strips of the patches*

4 Press the seams open.

5 The long strips are then joined, seaming the long edges of the oblongs together. The seams are positioned as the joints in brickwork (*fig. 130*).

Fig. 130 *Join the long edges to form a brick design*

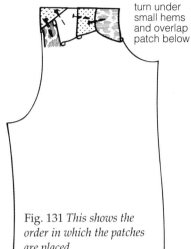

turn under
small hems
and overlap
patch below

Fig. 131 *This shows the order in which the patches are placed*

Once you have tried these simple patchwork shapes you will easily progress to more complicated designs.

Victorian crazy patchwork

This type of patchwork is made by sewing random shapes to a backing fabric. A layer of wadding may be used between the backing fabric and the patches. The patches are then sewn and quilted simultaneously. Crazy patchwork often has embroidery, lace, beads or ribbon added to the patchwork.

The patches may be sewn down using a variety of stitches. Satin stitch (see under Stitches, p. 91) gives a bold outline to the patchwork and if it is sewn using black thread the patchwork looks like 'stained glass'. Normally one colour thread is used throughout. It usually matches the most predominant colour in the patchwork.

Feather stitch and other machine embroidery stitches can also look very effective. Experiment with the stitches on your machine.

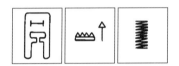

1 Set the machine as shown.

2 Cut the fabric into irregular shapes, some small, some large. Use both plain and patterned, dark and light fabrics.

3 Cut the backing fabric to the size required. This can be cut from a paper pattern if you are making a garment. (Cut the wadding to size if applicable).

4 Pin the first patch to the backing fabric, in the top left hand corner.

5 Fold under a small hem along one edge of the second patch and pin in place just overlapping the first patch. The next patch with one edge turned under overlaps the second patch, and is pinned in place (*fig. 131*). Continue turning under hems overlapping patches and pinning them to the backing fabric until the shape is completely covered. Vary the size of the patches and the direction of the stitching lines (*fig. 132*).

6 Stitch along the edges of the patches, using the stitch of your choice, until all have been sewn in place (*fig. 133*).

Try to put pale coloured fabric underneath dark colours when pinning the patches in place. If they are used the other way round the edges of the dark fabric sometimes show through the paler colours.

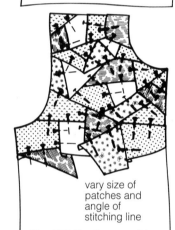

vary size of
patches and
angle of
stitching line

Fig. 132 *Continue patching until the backing fabric is completely covered*

Fig. 133 *Stitch along the edges of the patches*

PIPING

Piping is a decorative edging set in a seam. There are several methods of piping.

PIPING USING A BIAS STRIP ENCLOSING A CORD

Strips of fabric are cut on the bias (see under Bias Binding, p. 11), wide enough to cover a piping cord and allowing for a seam on both edges. Diagonal seams are sewn joining the short edges of the strips together. The thickness of the piping cord is dependent on the size of the garment or item to be piped, e.g. a thin cord would be used on a child's garment whereas a chunky cord would be used on loose covers. (Some cords will need to be washed – they are not all pre-shrunk.)

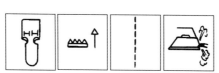

1 Set the machine as shown.

2 Fold the bias strip over the cord with the wrong side of the strip lying against the cord (*fig. 134*). (You may prefer to stitch the cord in place before proceeding.) Pin in place on the right side of the main fabric raw edges together.

3 Stitch the enclosed cord in place with the foot as close as possible to the cord (*fig. 135*).

4 Lay the two pieces of main fabric together – right sides facing with the enclosed cord between them.

5 Stitch them together on the same line of stitching.

Piping a cushion cover

1 Set the machine as shown for Method 1.

2 Always leave a long end 10 cm (4 in) of piping cord and fabric at the starting point. Begin sewing halfway down one side of the front (never at a corner). Attach the piping to the right side of the cushion

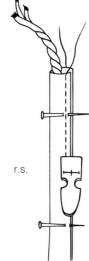

r.s.

Fig. 134 *You may find it easier to stitch the cord into the bias strip first*

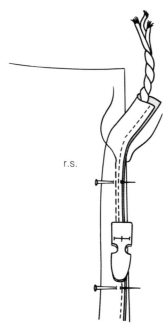

r.s.

Fig. 135 *Stitch the enclosed cord onto the main fabric*

front as described in Method 1. Sew along all sides, as close to the cord as possible, rounding off the corners, and stopping at least 10 cm (4 in) from the starting point (*fig. 136*).

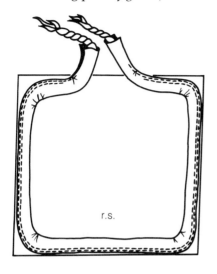

r.s.

Fig. 136 *Stop 10 cm (4 in) from the starting point and remove the work from the machine*

Fig. 137 *Cut, pin and sew a crosswise seam in the bias binding to fit the space*

Fig. 138 *Cut and splice the cord to fit the gap*

3 Remove the cushion front from the machine. Pin the bias strip to fit the remaining space to be sewn. Make a crosswise seam in the strip, cut off the excess fabric and press the seam open (*fig. 137*). Cut and splice the cord to fit the gap, wrapping the joined edges with sewing thread to secure (*figs. 138-139*).

Fig. 139 *Join the spliced ends of the cord by wrapping with thread*

4 Pin the bias strip over the cord and stitch in place. The front of the cushion now has a continuous piping round the edge (*fig. 140*).

5 Place the two pieces of cushion fabric together with right sides facing enclosing the piping. Pin in place and stitch together from the wrong side of the front, stitching on top of the existing line of stitching. Remember to leave an opening either in the back of the cushion cover or along one side to insert the pad!

Fig. 140 *The front of the cushion now has a continuous piping around the edge*

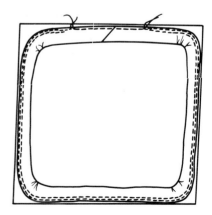

TO PIPE USING RUSSIA BRAID

A description of Russia Braid appears under Braids (p. 16). Russia braid, when sewn in a seam, forms a narrow piping cord and gives a silky outline to the seam. It is obtainable in a variety of colours and is a quick and easy way to add interest. It lays well on a curve so is ideal for piping collars etc. Once you have tried this easy form of piping I am sure you will use it often.

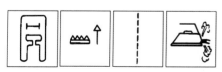

1 Set the machine as shown.

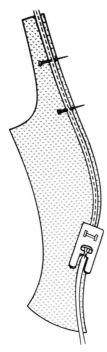

Fig. 141 *Sew in place on the right side of the fabric on the seam line. Stitch down the central groove of the braid*

2 Lay the braid on the seam stitching line on the right side of the fabric. Pin if necessary.

3 Sew in place, stitching along the central groove in the braid (*fig. 141*).

4 Place the two pieces of fabric to be seamed together, right sides facing. (The braid will now be laying between the two fabrics).

5 Sew exactly over the existing stitching attaching the braid, through all layers (*fig. 142*).

6 Press the seam (*fig. 143*).

TO PIPE RICK-RACK BRAID

Rick-rack braid forms a tiny scalloped edge outlining the seam. The method for sewing is the same as for Russia braid, but step 3 should now read: sew down the centre of the braid (*fig. 144*).

There are also many other types of piping cords available which do not need enclosing in fabric. They are already coloured (some are patterned) and they come in a variety of thicknesses and finishes, e.g. some are smooth and silky, whilst others have a dull finish. Many of these decorative cords have a small strip of flat fabric attached to one side for enclosing in a seam.

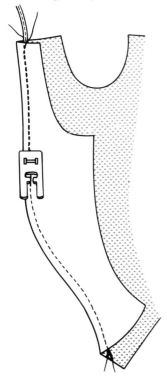

Fig. 142 *Sew exactly over the existing stitching*

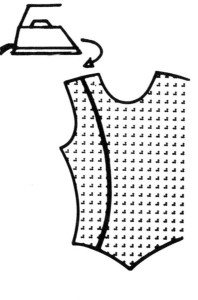

Fig. 143 *The seam is pressed open exposing the braid*

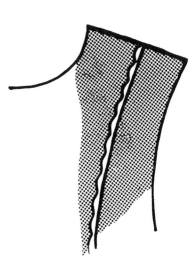

Fig. 144 *A decorative seam piping using rick-rack braid*

PRESSURE CONTROL

PRESSURE CONTROL EXPLAINED

When the take-up lever is lowered, pressure is exerted on the foot, which in turn presses onto the fabric regulating its flow through the machine. There are occasions when this pressure needs to be increased or reduced. If you are working on a very thin, slippery fabric it will require extra pressure to travel forward under the foot. Conversely, thicker fabrics will require a reduced pressure to travel freely under the foot.

When quilting or sewing down appliqué shapes a light pressure only is required because you will need to turn the fabric easily to follow the outline of the design, so the pressure will be reduced. Always slacken off the pressure when using wadding or when sewing across thick seams. When you are sewing on stretch fabrics the pressure also needs to be reduced because a strong pressure would press onto the fabric causing it to stretch as it was sewn, and the seams and hems would appear wavy.

CHANGING THE PRESSURE

The control to alter the pressure varies with different machines. Some machines have a silver knob on the top, above the presser-bar which has a silver band round it. If you press the band downwards the knob 'pings up', reducing the pressure on the foot. The knob can be pushed downwards to increase the pressure. There is usually a line marked on the side of the knob for normal sewing.

Your machine may have a numbered dial on the left hand side above the needle. (*Do not* confuse this with the tension dial which is usually on the front). The lower the number the lower the pressure. On some machines the top left hand side of the machine swings open to reveal a numbered dial – again, this is the pressure control and the lower numbers decrease the pressure.

Some of the newer machines have automatic pressure control, and the machine automatically adapts to different thicknesses. This is fine except when you need a light pressure in order to manipulate your material, e.g. when quilting, sewing patchwork or appliqué. For this reason I would prefer a machine with a manual control.

QUILTING

English quilting normally consists of three layers arranged as a sandwich, i.e. two layers of fabric enclosing a layer of wadding. An all-over design is then stitched through all layers. Quilting is lightweight, warm and decorative and can be used for bedspreads, cushions, jackets and waistcoats.

If necessary pre-shrink the fabrics before use. Quilting slightly reduces in size when it is worked so always cut your pattern out larger to compensate for this. Terylene wadding, which is now fireproof, is the most satisfactory filling because it is light and washes well. It also comes in different thicknesses (weights). If you are uncertain which thickness to buy, buy the thinnest, as it is easier to double up than to try to split a thicker weight.

The effect of the quilting is more pronounced if the backing fabric is heavier than the top fabric. Use a nonslippery backing fabric for bedcovers. Garments can be backed and then lined if necessary.

DESIGN

The easiest way to start quilting is to choose a patterned top fabric and quilt round the printed design, but remember that a small design will be more exacting to sew. It is possible to use a patterned fabric as the backing fabric with a plain coloured top fabric, sewing the quilting upside down from the back. The design on the backing fabric is automatically transferred to the plain top fabric.

Quilting templates can be purchased to help draw and plan your designs. You may wish to draw a freehand design on tracing paper and transfer it onto the fabric using dressmakers' carbon paper (for instructions see under Cutwork, p. 25).

Keep the design simple. Do not use too much stitching on your design because over-stitching flattens the quilting. The design is transferred onto the top fabric before the sandwich is assembled.

Another alternative is to sew a geometric design using the quilting guide to keep the lines parallel and equidistant. Set the distance between the needle and the quilting guide to correspond with the distance required between the lines of stitching. Start sewing on the right side of the work, on the extreme right hand side of the fabric. Always stitch in the same direction, e.g. from top to bottom. Each newly sewn line of stitching is moved to the right and fed under the quilting guide.

Having chosen a design the three layers of the sandwich need to be thoroughly smoothed out and pinned together before sewing. I find tacking threads get tangled up in the foot of the machine so I prefer to use pins. Where possible start sewing in the centre first and work outwards, though this is not possible if you are stitching a geometric design, in this case start at one edge and work methodically across the fabric.

There is now a slightly padded Vilene available which is marked with diamonds. It is ironed onto the back of the fabric and the diamond shapes can then be stitched from the back of the work giving a slightly quilted effect.

If you are making a large item you may find quilting easier to handle if it is worked in small sections which can be pieced together later. Quilting is usually sewn with a longer stitch and often with a thicker thread (see under Threads, p. 98). Because of the thickness involved the pressure on the foot will need reducing to allow the quilting to feed freely through the machine.

If you have problems following the outlines of your design because the foot obliterates the lines, you may wish to adapt a plastic foot (see under Tips No. 10, p. 100).

Method

 (optional)

1 Set the machine as shown. (The quilting guide is only necessary for geometric designs).

2 Transfer your design onto the right side of the top fabric.

3 Cut the wadding and backing fabric to fit.

4 Pin the three layers together smoothing them out from the centre.

5 Lengthen the stitch. Sew round your design through all layers (*fig. 145*).

NOTE:

You may like to experiment using other stitches. Stretch straight stitch may be used and gives a bold finish to the design.

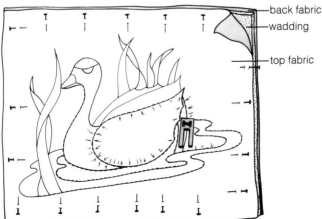

back fabric
wadding
top fabric

Fig. 145 *Sew round your design through all layers*

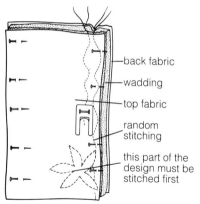

back fabric
wadding
top fabric
random stitching
this part of the design must be stitched first

Fig. 146 *Random quilting in progress*

Fig. 147 (Right) *The quilting is completed*

Fig. 148 (Far Right) *The quilting has been bound and lined to form a bag. The flower design has been painted with fabric paint and tiny beads have been added by hand*

RANDOM QUILTING

Random quilting is a quick and effective way of quilting. A sandwich is prepared as for English quilting and random wavy lines are sewn in rows from top to bottom (*figs. 146-147*). Always stitch in the same direction and remember that you do not need to draw the design on the top fabric first. Random quilting looks effective when sewn with stretch straight stitch or when using metallic thread. It can be highlighted with fabric paint and beads (*fig. 148*).

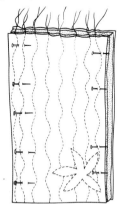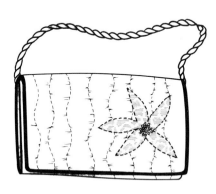

FREE STITCH QUILTING

This is a method of quilting which I use quite often. The design is very pronounced because the background is completely flattened with stitching.

Method

Mark the design on the right side of the top fabric using dressmakers' carbon paper. (At this stage I sometimes colour the drawn shapes with fabric paint). Cut a layer of wadding and a piece of backing fabric and pin together round the edges to form a sandwich, e.g. top fabric, wadding, bottom fabric.

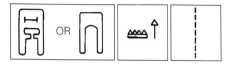

1 Set the machine as shown.

2 Lengthen the stitch slightly and stitch round the design.

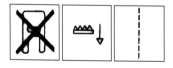

3 Set the machine as shown.

4 Completely cover the background, between the outlined shapes, with stitching. I usually stitch in very small clockwise whirls and circles, stitching right up to the stitching outlining the design (*fig. 149*). This heavy stitching depresses the background, and the design stands out in high relief. A shaded thread used to flatten the background looks very effective. Keep your fingers well clear of the needle area when manipulating the fabric sandwich. (A hoop is not necessary when sewing through wadding).

all straight stitching outlining the design must be worked first

TRAPUNTO QUILTING

This is a decorative form of quilting, not designed for warmth as only small areas are padded. An outline design is stitched through two layers of fabric (*fig. 150*). The back fabric behind the design is then slit open and the design is raised by stuffing through the slit (*fig. 151*). The slit is then hand-stitched together (*fig. 152*).

free stitch in small clockwise circles

Fig. 149 *Outline the design with straight stitching, then free stitch in small circles to depress the background*

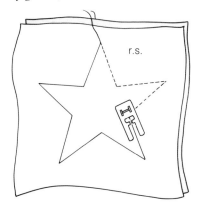

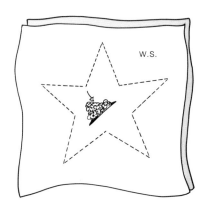

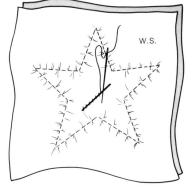

Fig. 150 *The outline of the design is stitched through two layers of fabric*

Fig. 151 *Make a slit in the design through the backing fabric only, and insert stuffing into the slit to raise the design*

Fig. 152 (Above) *Seal the slit with hand-stitching*

Fig. 153 (Below Left) *Stitch parallel rows using the double/twin needle*

ITALIAN QUILTING

Again, this type of quilting is purely decorative and consists of two layers of fabric. The backing fabric is usually a fine fabric, e.g. muslin. The design consists of two parallel rows of stitching sewn through both layers to form channels. The channels are then filled from the back using cord or wool which is threaded in a blunt ended tapestry needle (*fig. 154*). The cord/wool raises the lines to make the design stand out in relief. An ideal way to sew the narrow channels for Italian quilting is to use a twin needle. The two rows are then sewn simultaneously (*fig. 153*). Simple designs are most effective, using straight lines and large curves.

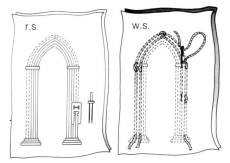

Fig. 154 *Fill the channels formed by threading wool through them from the back of the work*

ROULEAU

Rouleau is a narrow hollow tube of bias fabric used in dressmaking. Rouleau loops are often used as a decorative alternative to sewn buttonholes. They can be used on sleeve or neck openings where no underlap of fabric is necessary, or to fasten a bodice or jacket. Rouleau also has many other uses:

- For 'shoe string' shoulder straps

- A single or double strand makes a simple tie belt

- Several strands plaited together make a wider belt or strap

- For decorative neck fastenings by sewing loops down both sides of the neck opening and lacing them together using a length of rouleau

- For decorative bows

MAKING A ROULEAU TUBE

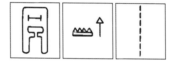

1 Set the machine as shown.

2 Cut narrow strips of bias fabric (see under Bias Binding, p. 11), approximately 2.5 cm (1 in), the finer the fabric the narrower the strip.

3 These strips may be seamed together along the short edge if a long length is required. (With right sides facing make a crosswise seam, trim and press open).

4 Make the tube by folding the strip of fabric in half (lengthways) with right sides together. Stitch approximately 6 mm from the fold, and reverse to fasten off (*fig. 155*). (If your machine needle can be set in several positions you may find it easier to move the needle across, so the distance between the needle and the edge of the foot is 6 mm. You can then line the fold up with the edge of the foot).

5 When you remove the fabric from the machine leave a long length of thread.

Fig. 155 *Stitching a rouleau tube*

6 Trim the raw edges leaving a narrow seam allowance.

7 Thread a blunt ended sewing needle with the long threads left at the end of the stitching. Tie the ends of thread to the eye of the needle and drop the needle down the tube and out at the bottom.

8 Pull on the threads and the tube will turn inside out.

9 Do not press the rouleau tube.

A special tool can be purchased for turning a rouleau tube. It is a long metal handle with a closing hook on the end. Use as follows:

1 Insert the handle into the tube of fabric.

2 Fasten the hook into the top of the tube and close.

3 Pull the handle out of the tube, thus turning the rouleau.

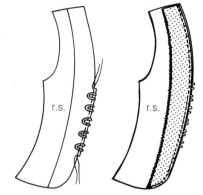

Fig. 156 *Stitch loops onto the right side of the garment (with the seam of the rouleau to the inside of the loop)*

Fig. 157 *Stitch the front and front facing right sides together*

ROULEAU BUTTON LOOPS

1 Make the rouleau tube as described. Allow twice the width of the button plus 4 cm (1½in) for seam allowances for each loop.

2 Position the loops in place on the right side of the garment; with the seams in the tube facing inwards, and stitch (*fig. 156*).

3 Stitch the facing in place and press to the wrong side of the garment (*fig. 157*). The loops will turn over ready for use (*fig. 158*).

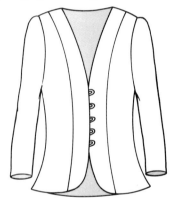

Fig. 158 *The finished loops protrude neatly from the jacket front*

TO MAKE A DECORATIVE ROULEAU PLAIT

1 Cut the bias strips from several different coloured fabrics.

2 Join the short lengths together to make a multi-coloured long strip (*fig. 159*).

Fig. 159 *Join short lengths of different coloured/patterned fabrics together using crosswise seams*

Fig. 160 *Plait several strands of multi-coloured rouleau together. The colours and fabrics will change along the length of the plait*

3 Make the rouleau as previously described.

4 Plait several strands of rouleau together. As the plait is made the colours will change along the length of the plait (*fig. 160*).

The plait can be used as a decorative belt, strap or braid.

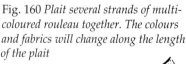

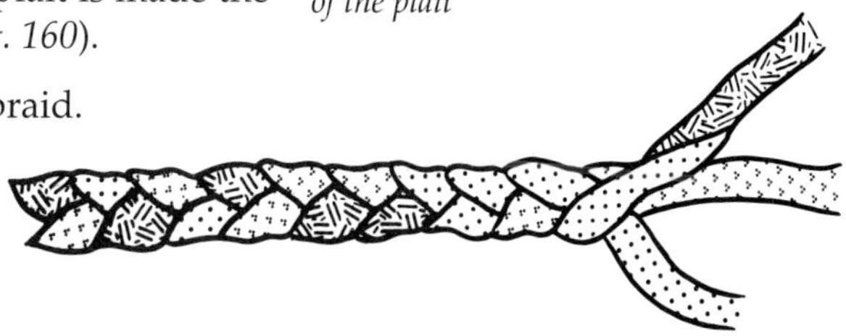

SEAMS

With the variety of neatening and strengthening stitches now available on modern sewing machines many types of seam are no longer needed. I am, therefore, only mentioning a few.

All the seams described below will use the machine setting as shown above.

FLAT SEAM

This is by far the most commonly used and can be used on a large variety of fabrics.

Method

1 Set the machine as shown. Set the stitch length to suit the fabric: the finer the fabric the shorter the stitch. (For fine or slippery fabrics see under Difficult Fabrics, p. 28)

2 Pin or tack the two layers together, right sides facing, raw edges parallel (*fig. 161*).

3 Stitch using straight stitch, leaving a seam allowance of approximately 1 cm.

4 Neaten the raw edges with zig-zag or three step zig-zag stitch.

5 Press the seam open to lay flat (*fig. 162*). (If the seam is made on a curve, the seam allowance will have to be clipped at intervals, to the stitching line, in order for it to be pressed open).

FRENCH SEAM

This is a neat self-finishing seam. It is used mainly on fabrics which fray badly or on sheer fabrics where the seam allowance would show through to the right side. It is often used on lingerie. Avoid this seam on curves, and use a mock French seam instead.

Fig. 161 *Pin and stitch the two layers of fabric together right sides facing, raw edges parallel*

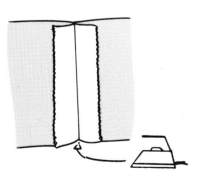

Fig. 162 *Zig-zag the raw edges and press the seam open*

Method

1 Set the machine as shown previously.

2 Sew the seam, with wrong sides facing and raw edges parallel, using straight stitch.

3 Trim the seam allowance to 3 mm and press the seam (*fig. 163*).

4 Turn and with the right sides facing press a fold along the seam line (*fig. 164*).

5 With straight stitch, and from the wrong side sew another row of stitching approximately 4 mm from the pressed fold (*fig. 165*). (This line of stitching should just encase the cut edges). Press.

LAP SEAM

This seam is used when joining fabrics which do not fray, e.g. felt or leather.

Method

1 Set the machine as shown previously.

2 Lay the two edges, right sides uppermost, overlapping each other facing in opposite directions. Pin or glue in place.

3 Work one row of straight stitching from the right side (*fig. 166*) and a second parallel row from the wrong side (*fig. 167*).

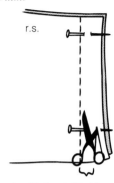

Fig. 163 *With wrong sides together and raw edges parallel pin and stitch the seam. Remove the pins and trim the seam width to 3 mm.*

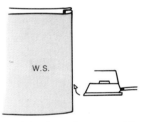

Fig. 164 *Turn and with the right sides facing press a fold along the seam line*

Fig. 165 *Stitching from the wrong side, sew another row of stitching 4 mm from the pressed fold. (This line of stitching should just encase the cut edges*

NOTE:

If you are stitching leather do not forget to use a leather needle, and to lengthen the stitch.

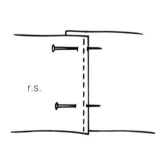

Fig. 166 *Lay the two edges overlapping each other, facing in opposite directions, and stitch in place*

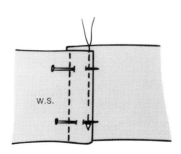

Fig. 167 *Work a second parallel row of stitching from the wrong side*

MOCK FRENCH SEAM

This seam is an easier version of a French seam. It may be used on the same types of fabric. Its main difference is that it can be used for a curved seam.

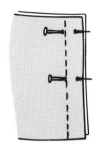

Fig. 168 *Sew a flat seam with right sides facing*

Method

1 Set the machine as previously shown.

2 Sew as for a flat seam with right sides facing (*fig. 168*). (See under Flat seam).

3 Fold the raw edges of the seam allowance to the inside and press.

4 Stitch together along the pressed edge (*fig. 169*).

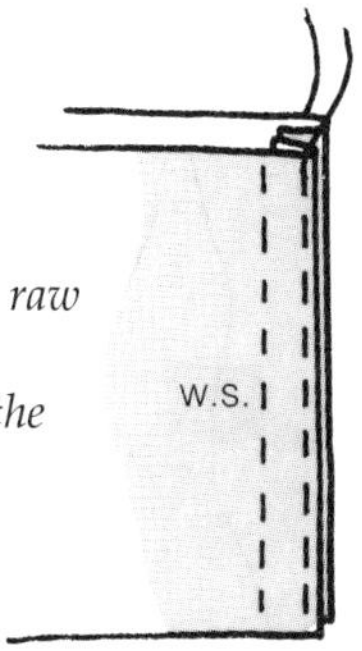

RUN AND FELL SEAM (FLAT FELLED SEAM)

This is a strong, self-finishing, flat seam which can look decorative. It is used on jeans and shirts. This type of seam is also worked on reversible garments since either side of the seam can be used as the right side.

Method

1 Set the machine as previously shown.

2 With wrong sides together sew a flat seam (*fig. 170*) (see under Flat Seam, p. 82).

3 Press the seam to one side (*fig. 171*).

4 Trim the underneath seam allowance to half its width (*fig. 172*).

5 Turn under a narrow hem on the wide seam allowance and press in place (*fig. 173*).

6 Stitch a line of straight stitching on the hem, close to the pressed fold, through all thicknesses (*fig. 174*). This second row of stitching is sometimes sewn in a contrast colour with a longer stitch length to give a decorative finish to the seam.

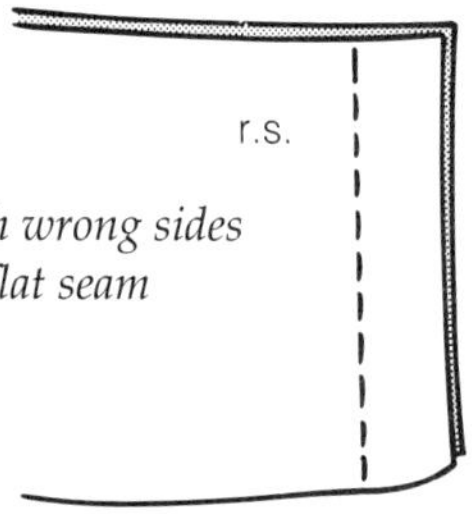

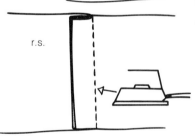

Fig. 169 *Fold in the raw edges of the seam allowance, press to the inside, and stitch*

Fig. 170 *With wrong sides facing sew a flat seam*

Fig. 171 *Press the seam to one side*

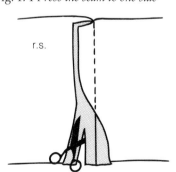

Fig. 172 *Trim the underneath seam allowance to half its width*

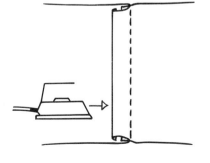

Fig. 173 *Turn under a narrow hem on the seam allowance and press in place*

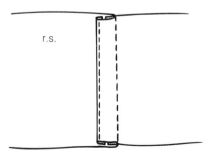

Fig. 174 *Stitch a line of stitching close to the pressed fold through all thicknesses*

Smocking

Smocking can be used on garments or soft furnishings to decrease fullness. It can also be used purely as a decorative finish. Three types of smocking are described below. The first method is the most practical and the other two methods are more decorative.

METHOD 1 – SMOCKING OVER GATHERS

At least twice the finished width of fabric is used for this method. Rows of long straight stitches are sewn approximately 1 cm (½ in) apart across the width of the fabric. The gathers are then pulled up to the required width and decorative stitching is sewn over the gathers.

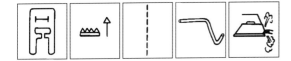

1 Set the machine as shown.

2 Set the stitch length to maximum.

3 Set the distance between the needle and the quilting guide to approximately 1 cm (½ in). (As this spacing is quite narrow, you may prefer to use the edge of the foot as a guide).

4 With the right side facing sew the first row of stitches on the right-hand edge of the fabric, lining up the cut edge with the quilting guide or foot.

5 Move the first row of stitching to the right and feed under the quilting guide or foot. Continue to stitch in rows across the width of the fabric using the quilting guide or foot to keep the rows of stitching parallel and equidistant.

6 When sufficient rows have been sewn for the depth of smocking needed, pull up the bobbin threads (*fig. 175*), to the finished width required (it is easier to do this in pairs), and tie off.

Distribute the gathers evenly along the width of the fabric and pull downwards to straighten the gathers. They are now ready for smocking.

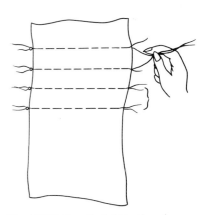

Fig. 175 *Pull up the bobbin threads*

Fig. 176 *Some suitable smocking stitches*

 zig-zag stitch

 zig-zag stitch sewn using a double needle

 stretch zig-zag stitch

stretch zig-zag stitch using a double needle

honeycomb stitch

feather stitch

double stretch overlock stitch

To Smock

Stitch rows of decorative stitches across the gathered fabric, *between* the long straight stitches. It is essential to stitch between the gathering threads, and not over them because this leaves them free to be pulled out when the smocking is completed. The stitches look better and have more elasticity if they are sewn on the longest and widest stitch settings.

Suggested Stitches

Zig-zag stitch could be used, (*fig. 176*) and it would be bolder if it was sewn using a twin needle. Stretch zig-zag is an ideal stitch to use and looks very impressive if sewn in contrasting colours, again with a twin needle. Honeycomb stitch is sometimes called smocking stitch. Feather stitch and double stretch overlock are other suitable stitches to use.

The stitches available obviously vary with the different machines. Make a test sample of gathering to try out some of the stitches on your machine.

When the rows of smocking are completed, steam the gathers in place (*fig. 177*). Hold a steam iron, above (not touching) the smocking, for a few seconds to 'set' the gathers. Pull out the gathering threads.

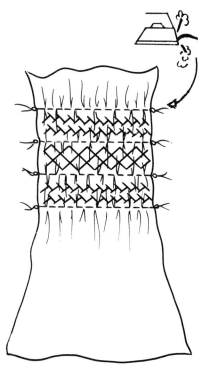

Suggested uses on garments	Suitable fabrics
Beneath the yoke of: a blouse a nightdress a childs' dress a lightweight coat	cotton lawn polycotton silk vyella brushed cotton
A narrow band of smocking can also be used to 'gather' up a frill or cuff	viscose polyester needlecord fine wool

Suggested uses on soft furnishings	Suitable fabrics
curtain headings the top and frill of a lamp shade a decorative panel in a cushion	chintz glazed cotton lightweight curtaining satin

Fig. 177 *A smocked section with the gathering stitches still in place, ready for steaming*

METHOD 2 – BEADED HONEYCOMB SMOCKING

This is a highly textured decorative method of smocking. It looks very rich when sewn on luxury fabrics, e.g. taffeta, satin, and silk. It is worked by sewing a grid of straight stitches. This stitching, unlike normal smocking, remains in the fabric. It forms part of the pattern, outlining the honeycomb shape. A contrast colour is usually used or a metallic thread can look very rich. Check that your machine will sew a metallic thread easily – there is a lot of stitching to do. (If you use a metallic thread use a normal thread on the bobbin). The squares and stitches are then 'pinched' together alternately with handsewn beads.

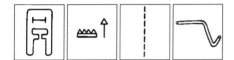

1 Set the machine as shown.

2 Set the distance between the quilting guide and the needle to 2.5 cm (1 in). (This setting is optional – it depends on the items being smocked). Usually, the smaller the item the smaller the grid). The setting used is suitable for an adult's waistcoat.

3 Set the stitch length to suit the fabric for normal sewing.

4 Starting at the right-hand side of the fabric sew lines of straight, parallel stitching using the quilting guide to keep them 2.5 cm (1 in) apart. Move each newly stitched line to the right.

5 When all the stitching in one direction is complete, turn the fabric round and stitch across in the other direction to form squares (*fig. 178*).

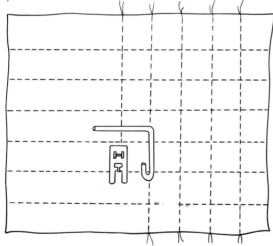

Fig. 178 *Stitching the grid, with the aid of the quilting guide, ready for beading*

6 Using small beads and handsewing, stitch on the right side as indicated.

7 For the following instructions, refer to *fig. 179*. Come up at A, take a small stitch at B, pass the needle through a bead and take a small stitch at A. Pull the thread closing A to B. Pass the needle back through the bead and down at B.

Fig. 179 *The beading sequence*

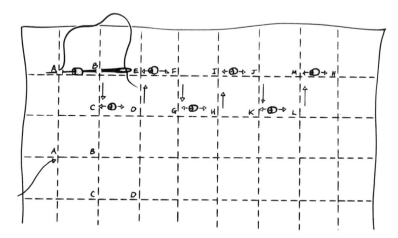

8 Slide the needle on the back down to C, come up at C. Take a small stitch at D, pass the needle through a bead and take a small stitch at C, then tighten the thread closing C to D. Do not pull the thread tight between B and C (the fabric between these two points must lie flat).

9 Pass the needle back through the bead and down at D. Take the thread across the back of the work and come up at E.

10 Close E to F as before, and so on, across the row of squares. When this row has been stitched, move down to the next row of squares and sew to form diamonds (*fig. 180*).

Fig. 180 *The completed smocking*

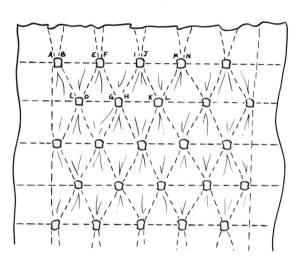

Suggested Uses	Suitable Fabrics
waistcoat fronts	silk
jacket yoke	satin
cushion front	taffeta
box top	velvet

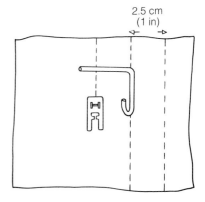

Fig. 181 *Sew the rows of stitching for the gathers using the quilting guide to keep them parallel and equidistant*

METHOD 3 – RIBBON SMOCKING

This is a decorative form of smocking. The fabric is prepared on the sewing machine. A double-sided satin 2 mm wide ribbon is threaded under and between the machine stitches by hand. (Between two and three times the finished width of fabric is the amount of ribbon used for each row). The fabric should be approximately three times as wide as the required finished width.

1 Set the machine as shown.

The stitch length is set just long enough to pull into gathers (not the very longest setting).

2 Set the distance between the needle and the quilting guide to 2.5 cm (1 in).

3 Start on the right-hand edge of the fabric, right side facing.

4 Line the cut edge up with the quilting guide. Stitch across the width of the fabric.

5 Continue stitching moving each newly stitched row to the right (*fig. 181*).

6 When all the rows have been stitched, start at the right-hand edge again and sew a second row of stitching alongside the first row using the width of the foot as a spacer. Repeat all the way across (*fig. 182*). You should end up with a narrow gap and a wide gap alternately.

7 Pull up the bobbin threads in pairs to the required width and tie off each end (*fig. 183*).

8 On the right side of the fabric, using the very narrowest 2 mm double-sided satin ribbon, thread a blunt ended tapestry needle, and slip the needle under the machine stitching, 'sewing' in zig-zags back and forth across the wide gap (*fig. 184*). (Do not sew through the fabric. Just slip the needle under the sewing threads).

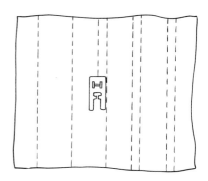

Fig. 182 *Sew the second row of stitching for the gathers using the edge of the foot to keep the rows parallel*

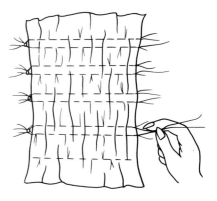

Fig. 183 *Pull up the bobbin threads in pairs and tie off*

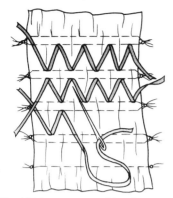

Fig. 184 *Lace narrow ribbon between the wide rows of stitching, using a blunt ended needle*

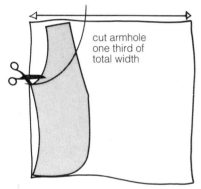

cut armhole one third of total width

Fig. 185 *Cut the armhole one third of the total width*

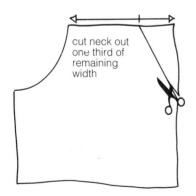

cut neck out one third of remaining width

Fig. 186 *Cut the neck one third of the remaining width*

Fig. 187 *When stitching is complete, lay the paper pattern over the fabric and pull up the gathers to fit the pattern*

The ribbon needs to be approximately two and a half times the width to lace across each row. Leave the small gaps, working only across the wide gaps.

A contrast colour stands out well, or you may prefer to smock in several colours.

A square or oblong piece of smocking is obviously the easiest shape to smock, but it is possible to smock a more complicated shape. If, for example, a waistcoat front needs to be smocked it should be cut out as follows:

For one front

1 Cut the length of fabric the same as the pattern. Cut the width three times as wide as the pattern. Cut the bottom of the armhole as indicated on the pattern, but cut the top of the armhole as follows:

2 Approximately one third of the shoulder is cut away on the pattern for the armhole, so cut one third of the fabric for the armhole as shown (*fig. 185*).

3 The front is also shaped at the neck edge and the amount cut away on the pattern is one third of the remaining shoulder width. So cut as shown (*fig. 186*).

4 When the machine stitching is complete lay the paper pattern onto the fabric and pull up the gathers to fit the paper pattern, then tie off the ends (*fig. 187*).

5 After the ribbon smocking has been completed, the waistcoat can be lined and the edges bound with crosswise strips of fabric. It is not necessary to smock the back of the waistcoat.

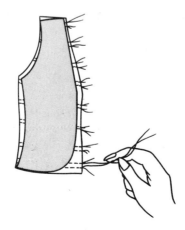

Suggested Uses

waistcoat
dress yokes
cushions
box tops
babies dresses

Suitable Fabrics

rich fabrics, e.g. silk, satin, taffeta. Cotton, polycotton, polyester, fine wool

STITCHES

Straight stitch (fig. 188)

Suggested uses:

- *General sewing (Seams and hems)* The finer the fabric to be sewn, the shorter the stitch length used.

- *Gathering* Use a long stitch length. (See Gathering, p. 48).

- *Top stitching* Lengthen the stitch slightly and possibly use a bolder (thicker) thread.

- *Free embroidery* (See under Embroidery, p.36)

- *Stay stitching* A line of straight stitching sewn along the edge of the fabric, before it is seamed, to prevent stretching. It is sewn with a slightly longer stitch length. If puckering occurs slacken off the top tension a little.

- *Tacking* A long straight stitch can be used as a tacking stitch to join seams ready for fitting.

Fig. 188 *Straight stitch*

Zig-zag (fig.189)

Suggested uses:
- *Neatening seams*

- *Attaching lace, bias binding and ribbon* It is much neater to attach ribbon and lace with a narrow zig-zag stitch.

- *Cord gathering* It can be used over cord to gather a thick or stiff fabric (See under Gathering, p.48).

- *Shirring* (See under Elastic, p.33).

- *Sewing seams on stretch fabrics* If you do not have stretch stitches on your machine, a very narrow zig-zag will seam stretch fabrics. It is particularly useful for sewing fine stretch fabrics. (Even if you have stretch stitches you may find them too heavy on finer fabrics). Do not forget to use a ball point needle and reduce the pressure.

Fig. 189 *Zig-zag stitch*

- *Satin stitch (fig. 190)* Set the stitch length to just above 0, the sideways sewn stitches should lay almost touching each other, forming a wide solid line. The fabric needs only light guidance as the machine will progress quite slowly. If you do not allow the fabric to feed freely through the machine a 'bump' of stitching will occur. If you push or pull the fabric through the machine the

Fig. 190 *Satin stitch*

density of the stitched line will be erratic. Try moving the width control as you sew, and the line of stitches will gradually taper and widen. This is a most versatile stitch with many uses, e.g. a bold line of satin stitch sewn on the hem of a tablecloth gives a professional finish. Satin stitch can be used to join patchwork, for appliqué, or as an embroidery stitch. It can wrap threads and outline shapes. Try using it with a shaded or multi-coloured thread.

Fig. 191 *Tapered bar tack*

● *Buttonholes and buttons* Zig-zag is used to sew buttonholes and for sewing on buttons. Consult your manual as methods vary with machines.

● *Tapered Bar-tacks (fig. 191)* Used above pleats for strengthening. (Alter the stitch width as you sew).

Three-step zig-zag (fig. 192)

Suggested uses:

Fig. 192 *Three-step zig-zag stitch*

● *Mending* Mending tears and darning threadbare patches (see under Darning, p. 27).

● *Neatening Seams* When using fine fabrics zig-zag stitch tends to curl the seam allowance into a ridge. If fine fabrics are neatened using three-step zig-zag the seam allowance remains flat. This stitch is also suitable for neatening stretch fabrics.

● *Attaching Flat Elastic* (See under Elastic, p. 32).

● *Ruching Braid* (See under Braid, p. 15).

Stretch stitching

A special foot can be used for sewing all stretch stitches except stretch straight stitch. A small bar lies down the middle of the foot and the stitches are sewn over the bar. Each stitch is therefore slightly looser than normal, giving it more elasticity.

Stretch straight stitch (fig. 193)

Suggested uses:

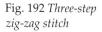

Fig. 193 *Stretch straight stitch*

● *Seaming stretch fabrics* (See under Stretch Fabric Sewing, p. 94).

● *Top stitching* This stitch is ideal for top stitching on all types of fabric. (The method is covered in more detail under Top stitching, p. 102).

● *Reinforcing* Stretch straight stitch is useful on all fabrics to reinforce areas of stitching which are subject to strain, e.g. round armholes and crotch seams. It is best to sew the seams, which need reinforcing, with a long straight stitch first. Then reinforce after fitting because stretch straight stitch is very difficult to unpick.

● *Quilting* Stretch straight stitch gives a bold outline when used for quilting.

Stretch zig-zag stitch (fig. 194)

Suggested uses:

- *Neatening Seams* Used on stretch fabrics.

- *Gathering* Can be used in conjunction with ribbon to gather fabric. (See instructions under Gathering, p. 49).

- *Decoration* This stitch can be used as a decorative top stitch.

Fig. 194 *Stretch zig-zag stitch*

Stretch overlock stitch (fig. 195)

Suggested uses:

- *Seaming and neatening* Used on sportswear this stitch seams and overlocks in one operation to produce a supple seam.

Fig. 195 *Stretch overlock stitch*

Satin stitch scallop (fig. 196)

Suggested uses:

- *Neatening Edges* When using this decorative stitch to neaten an edge there is no need to turn up a hem. Sew a line of scalloping about 2.5 cm (1 in) from the cut edge. (If you sew directly on the edge of the fabric it will be dragged down through the needle plate). Trim away the excess fabric with care using small sharp curved scissors. Painstaking, but worth it!

This method can be put to advantage when finishing the edge of a circular tablecloth where hemming on a curve would prove difficult. Scallops also make a decorative edging on collars and cuffs.

Fig. 196 *Satin stitch scallop*

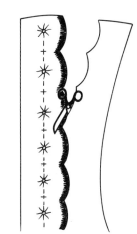

- *Broderie Anglaise Lace (fig. 197)* To ensure your lace matches your fabric you may like to make your own. Using cotton or polycotton fabric, cut into strips and join to form a long length. Scallop 2.5 cm (1 in) from the bottom edge, along its length. If your machine has embroidery stitches, select a stitch and sew a row just inside the scalloped edge. Trim away the excess fabric below the scallops. This can look especially effective if sewn with a wing needle using machine embroidery thread. Try using a shaded or multi-coloured thread.

Fig. 197 *Broderie Anglaise*

- *Decoration* Scallops can also be used for embroidery or as a top stitch.

Blind hem stitches

Suggested uses:

- *Hemming (fig. 198)* This is used when turning up a double hem.

- *Hemming (fig. 199)* This stitch is used when turning up a single hem because it neatens and hems in one operation.

Both of these methods are explained under Hems (p. 51).

Fig. 198 *Blind hem stitch for turning up a double hem*

Fig. 199 *Blind hem stitch for turning up a single hem*

STRETCH FABRIC SEWING

Stretch fabrics are popular because the garments made from them are very comfortable to wear. The garment 'gives' so movement is unrestricted. Stretch fabrics are widely used in the manufacture of sportswear.

Stretch fabrics are knitted, rather than woven and they require special treatment when they are sewn on the sewing machine.

TO SEW STRETCH FABRICS

1 Always use a ball point needle. These needles are available in different thicknesses and again the weight of the fabric is matched to the size of the needle. The finer the fabric, the thinner the needle. A ball point needle has a rounded tip which passes between the knitted fibres rather than piercing through them and eliminates the possibility of 'ladders' running from the seam line.

2 Use stretch stitches (see under Stitches, p. 92) when sewing stretch garments. These stitches have a degree of elasticity and allow the seam to 'give' with the fabric when the garment is worn. (If normal straight stitching is used it will restrict the movement of the garment and will eventually break when the garment is stretched. The seams will then come undone.) If you do not have stretch stitches on your machine try using a very narrow zigzag stitch instead of a normal straight stitch to sew up the seam. This will allow the seam to stretch when necessary.

3 All sideways sewn stitches e.g. zigzag or stretch overlock stitch, should be sewn using a stretch stitch foot on your machine. This foot looks like a general purpose zigzag foot, but it has a small raised bar running down the middle of the foot. The stitches are sewn over the bar which makes them slightly looser so that they are able to stretch with the fabric.

4 Always reduce the pressure on the foot (see under Pressure Control, p. 75). The fabric needs to pass smoothly under the foot without being stretched to avoid wavy seams.

5 Some stretch fabrics, usually those which have a dense shiny texture, prove very difficult to sew on the machine. The needle tends to bounce off the fibres without picking up the bobbin thread. Try using a perfect stitch needle, and if you have the facility to move the position of your needle, move it so that the stitches are sewn as close to the foot as possible. (Turn the balance wheel manually first, to check that the needle clears the foot.) When sewing a stretch straight stitch the straight stitch foot may help.

6 The stitch quality is better if you use a thread to match your fabric e.g. a polyester thread on a man-made fabric.

SPECIAL EFFECTS ON STRETCH FABRICS

Sewing a decorative hem

The stretchy nature of stretch fabrics can at times be used to advantage e.g. a decorative 'frilly' hem can be produced by stretching the fabric as it passes under the foot whilst stitching is in progress. (See under Lettuce Hem, p. 53)

Appliqué on stretch fabric

When applying a woven fabric onto a knitted fabric the knitted fabric needs to be stabilized to prevent it from stretching. Hand tack a piece of stitch-and-tear vilene to the wrong side of the knitted fabric where the appliqué is to be worked. Then follow the instructions for appliqué. (See under Appliqué, p. 8)

Machine embroidery on stretch fabrics

Machine embroidery can look very effective on stretch fabrics. Choose fabrics which are dense and have a smooth surface. Again, the fabric will need to be stabilised by hand tacking stitch-and-tear vilene to the wrong side to prevent it stretching whilst stitching the machine embroidery. (A hoop is not necessary when using stitch-and-tear vilene.)

Overlocking stretch fabrics

An overlocker is ideal for seaming and neatening manufactured stretch fabrics. It can also be used with success on hand and machine knitting. (See under Overlockers p. 66)

TENSION

Contrary to popular belief there is no great mystery about setting tensions and in practice it is not difficult. If your tension is poor then simply correct it as explained below.

The machine tension, correctly set so that the bobbin thread and top thread lock in the middle of the fabric, needs very little adjustment for the life of the machine. There are a few exceptions, however, e.g. when making pin tucks or sewing machine embroidery. For general sewing it is not necessary to frequently alter your tension. Modern machines are capable of sewing most fabrics with the same tension setting, and it is the needle size, pressure and the length of stitch which needs to be adjusted to suit the fabric, not the tension. As a general rule the thinner the fabric the shorter the stitch length.

Ignore books which say the bobbin tension never needs adjustment – if the tension is poor you must correct it.

Step-by-step method of setting tensions

1 Thread the bobbin with one colour thread and the top with a contrasting colour thread of the same thickness and manufacture.

2 Set the top tension indicator to the middle of its range, e.g. if the machine has a knob marked 0-9 set it between 4 and 5.

3 Use a small piece of medium weight fabric, e.g. cotton twill or calico, to test the tension by stitching a line of straight stitch and a line of zig-zag. (It is often easier to see if the tension is correct on zig-zag stitching).

4 Check to see if the threads are locking in the middle of the fabric (*fig. 200*). You should not be able to see any 'dots' of the bobbin colour on the top, or any 'dots' of the top thread on the underside of the stitching. The same applies to the zig-zag sample. If the two threads do not lock in the centre of the fabric correct the *bobbin* tension as below.

5 To *tighten* the bobbin thread. If the bobbin thread colour appears on the top of the fabric the bobbin thread is too loose and needs tightening by turning the screw on the bobbin case, or if your machine has a drop-in bobbin, turn the screw located to the side of the bobbin. (If *figs. 201-202* are not applicable to your machine, consult your manual). To tighten the bobbin tension, turn the screw clockwise with a small screwdriver. Try turning it a quarter turn at

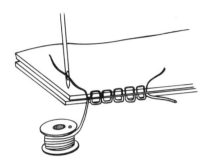

Fig. 200 *Good tension: the top and bottom threads lock in the middle.*

Fig. 201 *A 'front loading' bobbin case indicating the tension adjustment screw*

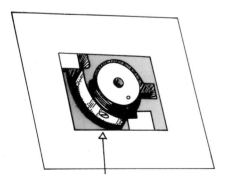

Fig. 202 *A 'drop-in; bobbin showing the tension adjustment screw*

a time and then sew a sample. It is a case of trial and error and you may need to tighten the screw in several stages before you get the threads to lock in the centre of the fabric.

6 To *loosen* the bobbin thread. If the top thread shows on the underside of the fabric the bobbin tension needs loosening. This can be achieved by turning the screw on the bobbin case, or for the drop-in bobbin, by turning the screw alongside the bobbin, anti-clockwise. Use a small screwdriver and try turning the screw a quarter turn at a time anti-clockwise. Then sew a sample of straight stitch and a zig-zag sample. You may need to adjust the screw several times until you are happy with the stitching. Occasionally, especially with an old, well used machine, the threads on the screw become worn and the bobbin case needs replacing.

Achieving a good tension with the top tension knob set in the middle of the dial allows room for adjustment. To increase the top tension turn the knob to a higher number, to decrease the top tension turn to a lower number. Adjustment is necessary when two different weight threads are being used, i.e. the top thread is a different thickness from the bobbin thread. For instance, if you were using a metallic thread on the top and a synthetic thread on the bobbin the top tension would need adjustment to balance the threads. The same would apply if a thin silky embroidery thread was being used on the top and a synthetic thread was wound on the bobbin.

Often when a block satin stitch is being sewn the top tension needs to be loosened. You will soon become familiar with altering the tension to achieve a good stitch quality but always remember to turn back to the middle of your dial for normal sewing.

NOTE:

If, whilst sewing, your stitching suddenly becomes erratic, do not reach for the tension knob! Look at the faults page. It is never the tension which needs adjusting.

THREADS

The selection of different types and makes of threads available can be rather confusing. However, most threads fall into one of the following categories:

Basic types

- *100% Polyester thread* Widely acclaimed, this was introduced as a 'sew all' fabrics thread, but since then some of the old favourites (such as cotton and silk) have been reintroduced.

- *100% Cotton thread* For stitching pure cotton.

- *Silk thread* For silk fabrics. It is surprising how thick this thread looks.

- *Cotton polyester thread* Another useful thread which can be used on mixture fabrics, e.g. polycotton.

Special purpose threads

- *Machine embroidery thread* Some makes are still numbered and some give you a choice of thickness in each colour – the lower the number the thicker the thread.

- *Rayon and viscose threads* These are suitable for embroidery and give a lovely shiny finish to the stitch. Some makes of thread come in multicolours, one colour merging into another colour on the same reel. Other reels have dark shades flowing into lighter shades of the same colour.

- *Metallic threads* These can be used on the machine, but I would choose a smooth thread in preference as they break and fray less easily. When using metallic thread on a garment wind normal thread on the bobbin. If you have problems with metallic threads breaking, try winding the metallic thread on the bobbin and sewing the work upside down.

The numbers denoting the thickness of the thread have, in general, been dropped as threads have become thinner and stronger, purpose made for fast machining. There is, however, a strong thick thread still produced for quilting and top stitching.

Cheaper threads of good quality are now coming onto the market from the Far East and the US – yet despite their price they generally sew well on the machine.

NOTE:

When using metallic thread on a garment wind normal thread on the bobbin, because metallic threads can irritate the skin.

TIPS

No. 1

If your machine has a knob on the balance wheel which you turn to stop the needle operating when winding the bobbin, always loosen this knob when you put the machine away. This ensures that it will operate freely when you need to use your machine again. I expect many of us have found this knob will not turn at times. It needs drastic action: a sharp tap with a wooden mallet or rolling pin in the centre of the knob will often release it.

No. 2

If your machine is not stitching well re-thread the bobbin, top thread, and change the needle. In nine out of ten cases the problem will be solved.

No. 3

When buying new bobbins, needles, or feet for your machine always take a sample of yours with you. This will ensure your purchases fit your machine when you get home. Also, some accessories fit several makes of machines, so you may have more choice if you have samples with you.

No. 4

To turn under a curve, e.g. the bottom curves of a patch pocket, sew a line of straight stitching on the fold line of the pocket and you will find the seam allowance folds neatly under (*figs. 203-204*). It can be pressed in place ready for stitching to the garment.

Fig. 203 *Sew a line of straight stitching on the fold line of the pocket*

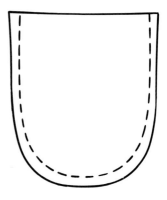

Fig. 204 *Clip and press, the curve will now turn under smoothly*

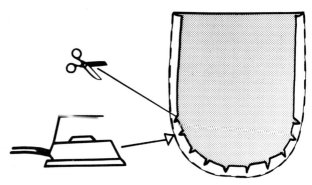

N o . 5

If your machine is new, or maybe you do not use it regularly, and you find it difficult to remember what the various knobs do – make yourself small sticky labels and stick them to the machine above the knobs, e.g. tension, width control (zig-zag), and stitch length. This saves time and familiarizes you with the machine.

N o . 6

When making buttonholes, start with the bottom one on a garment. They get better (and you get more confident) as you progress, so the top ones which show will be perfect!

N o . 7

Buy all your family a pair of scissors so that they are not tempted to use yours.

N o . 8

Always do your sewing first and your housework last. One will wait – the other will not. Much pleasure and satisfaction can be gained, for many years, from your sewing. The same cannot be said for housework, it will look just as bad next week!

N o . 9

Always have an iron set up when you are machining and press each seam after sewing. I find a travel iron situated on the right hand side of the machine works well.

N o . 1 0

When sewing along a line marking a design, e.g. when stitching appliqué or quilting, it can sometimes be difficult to see. Buy a spare plastic zig-zag foot and cut away the small bars which lie horizontally across the foot (*figs. 205-206*). This leaves a large opening and makes it easier to follow a line.

N o . 1 1

A full length mirror is also a must if you are making your own clothes.

N o . 1 2

One thing I have learned over the years is not to start a new project, however exciting it may be, until you have completed the one you are working on. It is easy to loose interest in something and put it away (perhaps for ever!). Also if you have made a mistake, however serious you think it is, do not put the piece away to sort out at a later date. It is quite often left there for good. Try to think of a way of correcting the mistake straight away. Who knows, because

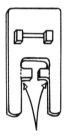

Fig. 205 *Cut away the sections of the plastic foot indicated by the arrows*

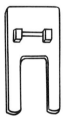

Fig. 206 *This leaves a wider opening in the foot and enables you to see your design more clearly whilst stitching is in progress*

you have given it more thought, it may turn out to be your best piece of work yet!

No. 13

When placing pins in your work, always place them across the seamline. The machine will then straight stitch over them (*fig. 207*).

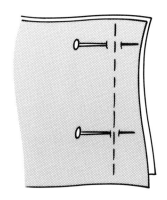

Fig. 207 *If pins are placed at right angles to the stitching line the machine will straight stitch over them*

No. 14

It is not always easy to know, when choosing a dressmaking pattern, if the style will suit you. Time, money, and effort can often be wasted. Burda patterns provide a service which helps the home dressmaker overcome this problem. When you purchase your first Burda pattern you can send to Burda and receive a free quarterly magazine. These magazines have hints and tips as well as helpful advice on which pattern styles will suit your particular shape. There is guidance on which fabric to choose and lots of information on fashion trends and colours. A very worthwhile read.

No. 15

A thin rubber mat under the machine helps to stop vibration and prevents the machine from moving whilst you are sewing.

No. 16 – A hot tip!

Sewing a freehand perfect circle is very difficult and any slight wobble is instantly noticeable, but a perfect circle can be sewn every time using this very simple method:

1 Frame up your material.

2 Stick two short lengths of masking tape in a cross, roughly in the centre, on the back of the fabric.

3 Lay a drawing pin, point uppermost, on the flat bed of your machine to the left-hand side of the needle. The distance between the drawing pin and the needle will be half the width of the circle (the radius).

4 Put a short length of masking tape over the point of the drawing pin sticking it in place on the bed of the machine.

5 Lay the framed fabric over the drawing pin so that the point protrudes approximately through the centre of the fabric.

6 Select a stitch (embroidery stitches work well) and start sewing. You will not need to hold or guide the frame. Just let it feed round on its own until the circle is completed. Hey presto a perfect circle!

TOP STITCHING

Top stitching gives a bold, eye-catching finish to a garment. In most cases it is sewn when the garment has been made up and well pressed. If you wish to sew more than one row of top stitching, using a straight or stretch straight stitch, it is advisable to use a twin or triple needle. The rows sewn will then be perfectly parallel. This would be difficult to achieve by eye with a single needle.

If a single row of stitching is required a special needle is available with an extra large eye. This is useful when using thicker thread.

Top stitching can be sewn in straight stitch, or if you prefer a bolder look, stretch straight stitch, (remember it does not unpick easily). Always lengthen your stitch for top stitching.

For a really bold top stitch, perhaps on a heavier fabric, use satin stitch. If this is not bold enough, try raised satin stitch. This is satin stitch sewn over a cord. A special attachment can be used to guide the cord under the foot, or a cording foot may be used.

For a more decorative top stitch try using embroidery stitches, either with a single, twin or triple needle. Also experiment with different threads. The combinations are endless!

TUCKS

Tucks are used to decrease fullness or length. They are usually worked in rows and follow the horizontal or vertical grain lines of the fabric.

PIN-TUCKS

As their name suggests these tucks are very narrow and they can be worked in several ways.

Method 1 – Using the twin needle

This is the easiest method of sewing pin-tucks and uses the twin needle. The height of the raised pin-tuck depends on the thickness of the fabric and the thread tension. The tighter the top tension, and the thinner the fabric, the more raised your tuck will be.

Try sewing a few experimental tucks, adjusting the tension, until you are happy with the results. (Always practice using the same fabric you will be working with later). Fine soft fabrics give a more pronounced tuck.

Work these tucks with the fabric laying flat under the foot (not along the edge of a fold). If the distance between the tucks is very narrow the edge of the foot can be used as a guide, but if a wider gap between them is required the quilting guide can be used. Either of these methods will keep the lines of tucks parallel and equally spaced. Always start by stitching the tuck on the extreme right and keep moving each newly stitched tuck to the right. Always stitch in the same direction, e.g. from top to bottom.

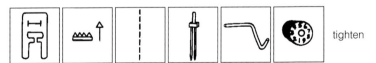 tighten

Fig. 208 *Sewing pin-tucks, on flat fabric using a twin needle and a quilting guide. (No folding is necessary)*

1 Set the machine as shown.

2 Draw a line on the right side of the fabric with a water or air-soluble pen where the first pin-tuck will be sewn. If you are using a dark fabric you may have to use tailors' chalk to draw the line.

3 Set the distance between the needle and the quilting guide to correspond with the distance between the pin-tucks. (The quilting guide is optional, as the edge of the foot could be used as a guide).

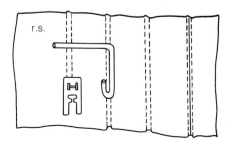
r.s.

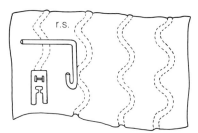

Fig. 209 *Curved pin-tucks using a twin needle and straight stitch scallop*

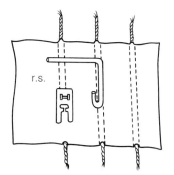

Fig. 210 *To raise pin-tucks even higher they can be sewn over a cord*

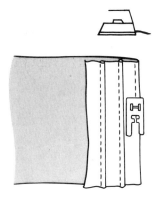

Fig. 211 *Press the pin-tucks before stitching, and use the edge of the foot as a guide to keep the spaces between them equal*

4 Sew the first pin-tuck following the drawn line. It is important to sew the first tuck straight, if there is a bend in it all the following tucks will have a bend in them!

5 Move the first pin-tuck to the right and line up with the right-hand edge of the foot or the quilting guide (*fig. 208*). Sew the second tuck, and so on, until all the tucks are sewn.

Curved pin-tucks make a more decorative pin-tuck and can be sewn with the twin needle using three step zig-zag or straight scallop stitch (*fig. 209*). For these stitches simply follow method 1 instructions for sewing twin needle pin-tucks.

Corded pin-tucks

These are made using the same method as for the twin needle pin-tucks above. A fine cord is sewn under the pin-tuck to raise it even higher (*fig. 210*). The cord is laid under the fabric along the line of the tuck. It helps the cord to stay in place if your presser foot has a groove down the centre of the underside. Stitch the tuck from the right side of the fabric, using a twin needle. The bobbin thread holds the cord in place.

Method 2 – Folded pin-tucks

1 Set the machine as shown.

2 Mark the position of the tucks. You may find it easier to press along the fold lines before sewing.

3 The first pin-tuck to be sewn is the one on the extreme left hand side of your fabric. Sew a line of stitching very close to the folded edge. Move the sewn pin-tuck to the left. The left hand side of the foot can then be used as a guide to keep the stitching straight on subsequent pin-tucks.

4 Repeat moving each pin-tuck to the left until all pin-tucks have been stitched (*fig. 211*).

LARGE TUCKS

These lay like stitched pleats and each flap covers the line of stitching holding the previous tuck. The quilting guide can be used to keep the stitching straight. The distance between the fold and the stitching line should be the same as the distance between the needle and the quilting guide.

Method

1 Set machine as shown.

2 On the right side of the fabric mark the position of the fold and the stitching line for each tuck.

3 *First tuck* – right side facing, and starting with the bottom tuck, press the fold and stitch through both layers along the stitching lines (*fig. 212*).

4 Press the stitched line open on the back of the fabric (*fig. 213*).

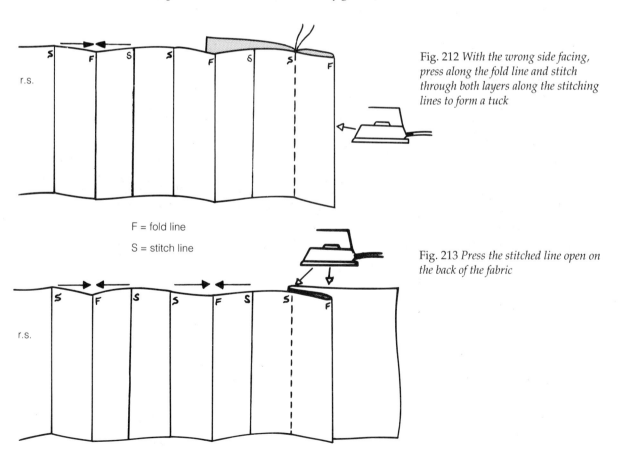

r.s.

F = fold line
S = stitch line

r.s.

Fig. 212 *With the wrong side facing, press along the fold line and stitch through both layers along the stitching lines to form a tuck*

Fig. 213 *Press the stitched line open on the back of the fabric*

5 *Second tuck* – press the second fold and stitch on the stitching lines. The first tuck will be folded back underneath (*fig. 214*).

6 Press open on the back after stitching. The stitched line on the first tuck should be covered by the fold on the second tuck, and so on until all the tucks are sewn (*fig. 215*).

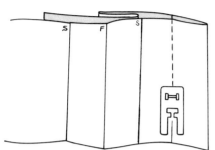

Fig. 214 *Stitch the second tuck, the first tuck will be folded back underneath*

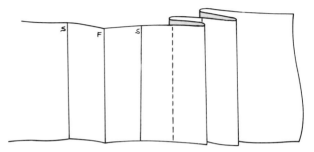

Fig. 215 *When pressed in place, each tuck covers the stitching line of the previous tuck*

N O T E :

Try sewing a row of machine embroidery stitches along each tuck (*fig. 216a*), or edge them with tiny hand stitched blanket stitches, slipping a small bead or pearl onto perhaps every third or fourth stitch. Tucks can also be sewn with a lace edging (see under Lace, p. 59).

A decorative textured fabric can be made by sewing rows of tucks (*fig. 216b*). Straight stitch is then sewn alternately at intervals up and down the rows of tucks, folding them backwards and forwards. (Use the quilting guide when sewing the parallel rows of straight stitching.)

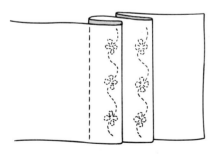

Fig. 216a *A decorative effect can be achieved by sewing machine embroidery stitches along each tuck*

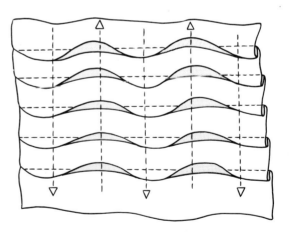

Fig. 216b *A decorative textured fabric made by sewing rows of tucks and then straight stitching, alternately up and down across them, turning the tucked edges backwards and forwards*

TWIN-NEEDLE SEWING

A twin-needle has a single shaft which pushes up into the machine and two needles which branch out from the shank (*fig. 217*). The gap between the needles may vary.

A triple needle may also be used but it is not so readily available (*fig. 218*). The instructions below can be adapted for use with a triple needle .

Threading up the machine

It is best to consult your manual for the threading up procedure when using a double needle. Usually, however, there are two spool-holders, and the two threads are separated before they go through the tension discs. They then travel on together before separating again when the needles are threaded.

If you only have one top spool-holder on your machine and it will not accommodate two reels of thread, try winding the thread onto spare bobbins and placing them one above the other (or side by side as the case may be) on the top spool holder. The bobbin is set up as for normal sewing.

Experiment with different threads. A subtle look can be achieved by using different shades of the same colour. Shaded or multi-coloured thread can be very effective, whereas two different colours can give a good contrast, especially if used for smocking.

Setting the dials

When using a twin-needle it is essential to use a general purpose (zig-zag) foot. *Never* set the width control wider than halfway, e.g. if your width control goes up to 6 the setting must not be set wider than 3. On some machines a picture of the twin needle will be drawn on the dial. At this point, do not turn the dial any further.

Electronic and computerized machines quite often have a button or pad with a picture of a twin needle above. When this is pressed the width is automatically set to accommodate a twin needle.

Before you start sewing always turn the balance wheel manually downwards and towards you, to check that the needles are not hitting the foot or needle plate.

Fig. 217 *A twin needle, (sometimes called a double needle) simultaneously sews two parallel lines of stitching*

Fig. 218 *A triple needle simultaneously sews three parallel lines of stitching*

NOTE:

If the width is set beyond halfway the needles will hit the foot or needle plate and they will break.

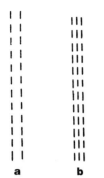

Fig. 219 *An example of straight stitching (a) using a twin needle and (b) using a triple needle*

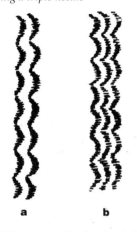

Fig. 220 *An example of satin stitch scallop (a) using a twin needle and (b) using a triple needle*

Stitches — suggestions for use:

Most stitches are suitable for twin needle stitching, but some of the more elaborate outline patterns can look rather over complicated.

Stitches	*Uses*
All Stitches	Decoration. (Block satin stitch patterns tend to look bolder.)
Straight Stitch (fig. 219)	Top stitching, pin-tucks, corded pin-tucks (See under Tucks, p. 103).
Stretch Straight Stitch	Top stitching (beware it is very difficult to unpick), smocking.
Stretch Zig-Zag	Smocking.
Scallop Stitch (fig. 220)	This produces a double scallop which can look very effective round a hem, especially on table linen.

ZIPS

This is an easy way of inserting a standard zip which guarantees success everytime.

METHOD 1

Use this method to insert a standard zip with an equal amount of fabric on each side. This type of insertion is normally used when sewing a zip into the centre back of a garment.

1 Set the machine as shown.

2 Sew the seam to the point where the bottom of the zip will be. Fasten off by reversing a short way. Leave the needle in the fabric.

3 Change the stitch length to the longest setting and continue up the seam to within 2.5 cm (1 in) of the top (*fig. 221*).

4 Press the seam open.

5 Pin, or pin and tack, the closed zip in position on the wrong side of the garment. Ensure that the zip teeth lay directly over the join (*fig. 222*).

6 Put the zip foot on the machine with the needle on the right-hand side of the foot.

7 Change the stitch length back to its original setting.

8 Sew the open zip in from the right side of the garment starting at the top on the left-hand side. Sew the first 2.5 cm (1 in) (not too close to the teeth), stop, lift the foot, close the zip, lower the foot and sew to the bottom of the zip leaving the needle in the fabric – then pivot (*fig. 223*).

9 Sew across the bottom of the zip leaving the needle in the fabric – then pivot again.

10 Sew up the other side, the same distance away from the seam, to within 2.5 cm (1 in) of the top. Lift the foot, slide the zip open past

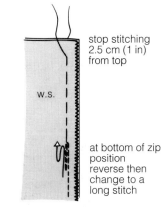

stop stitching 2.5 cm (1 in) from top

w.s.

at bottom of zip position reverse then change to a long stitch

Fig. 221 *Using a long straight stitch 'machine tack' the zip opening*

w.s.

Fig. 222 *The zip is tacked in place with the teeth exactly over the machine tacked seam*

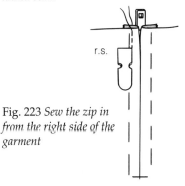

r.s.

Fig. 223 *Sew the zip in from the right side of the garment*

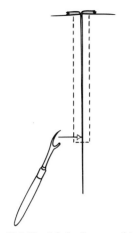

Fig. 224 *Unpick the long machine tacking stitches leaving the zip neatly covered*

Fig. 225 *Using the long straight stitch, machine tack the zip opening*

Fig. 226 *Tack the zip to the wrong side of the zip opening making sure the teeth lie to the right hand side of the seam*

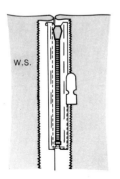

the foot, lower the foot and continue sewing to the top. Fasten off by sewing backwards a short way.

11 You can now easily unpick your long stitches (machine tacking) from the seam in front of the zip and your fabric will meet evenly over the zip (*fig. 224*). Wonderful!

METHOD 2

Use this method to insert a standard zip as a lapped zip, where one side of the zip has a wider flap which laps over the zip teeth. This method of insertion is used when sewing a zip into the side seam of a garment. The wide flap faces towards the back of the garment.

1 Set the machine as shown.

2 Sew the seam to the point where the bottom of the zip will be. Fasten off by reversing a short way. Leave the needle in the fabric.

3 Change the stitch length to its longest setting and continue up the seam to within 2.5 cm (1 in) of the top (*fig. 225*).

4 Press the seam open.

5 Pin or pin and tack the closed zip to the wrong side of the garment, with the teeth just to the right-hand side of the zip seam (*fig. 226*).

6 Put the zip foot on the machine with the needle on the right-hand side of the foot.

7 Turn the stitch length knob back to its original setting.

8 Sew the zip in from the wrong side starting from the top of the left-hand side. The first 2.5 cm (1 in) of the zip will need to be open initially. Proceed to sew close to the teeth (*fig. 227*). When 2.5 cm

Fig. 227 *Sew the zip in from the wrong side*

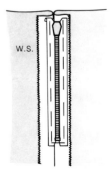

(1 in) has been sewn lift the foot up and slide the zip closed. Put the foot down and continue to sew to the bottom of the zip leaving the needle in the fabric – then pivot.

9 Sew across the bottom, leave the needle in the fabric, then pivot again. Turn and sew up the other side of the zip right to the top. This time the sewing line should be close to the outside edge of the zip tape.

10 Unpick the large stitches from the seam in front of the zip and you should have a perfect lapped zip (*fig. 228*).

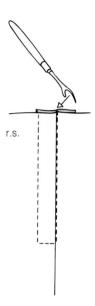

r.s.

Fig. 228 *Unpick the long machine tacking stitches leaving the lapped zip neatly covered*

NOTES

If any ideas or tips occur to you whilst you are sewing you may like to jot them down on this page for easy reference.